P9-BZV-810

Renewal
as a Way of Life

A Guidebook
for Spiritual Growth

Richard F. Lovelace

INTERVARSITY PRESS
DOWNERS GROVE, ILLINOIS 60515

InterVarsity Press is the book-publishing division of Inter-Varsity Christian Fellowship, a student movement active on campus at hundreds of universities, colleges and schools of nursing. For information about local and regional activities, write IVCF, 233 Langdon St., Madison, WI 53703.

All scriptural quotations, unless otherwise noted, are taken from the Revised Standard Version of the Bible, copyrighted 1946, 1952, © 1971, 1973. All scriptural quotations noted NIV are taken from the Holy Bible: New International Version, copyright © 1973, 1978, International Bible Society; used by permission of Zondervan Bible Publishers. All scriptural quotations noted NASB are from the New American Standard Bible, © The Lockman Foundation 1960, 1962, 1963, 1968, 1971, 1972, 1973, 1975, 1977.

The excerpt from W. H. Auden's poem "For the Time Being: A Christmas Oratorio" that appears on p. 27 is from W. H. Auden: Collected Poems, ed. Edward Mendelson, © 1944 and renewed 1972 by W. H. Auden, and used by permission of Random House, Inc.

Distributed in Canada through InterVarsity Press, 860 Denison St., Unit 3, Markham, Ontario L3R 4H1, Canada.

Cover illustration: John Walker

ISBN 0-87784-594-8

Printed in the United States of America

Library of Congress Cataloging in Publication Data
Lovelace, Richard F.

  Renewal as a way of life.

  Bibliography: p.
  1. Spiritual life. I. Title.
BV4501.2.L67   1985   248.4   85-10029
ISBN 0-87784-594-8

17	16	15	14	13	12	11	10	9	8	7	6	5	4	3	2	1
99	98	97	96	95	94	93	92	91	90	89	88	87	86	85		

This book is for
Grover and Helen Willcox,
who taught me the connection
between spiritual renewal
and a pastor's heart.

Preface

This work began as a response to requests for a simplified version of my earlier book *Dynamics of Spiritual Life* (IVP). Many wanted something more suitable for students and lay readers with a modest theological background. But *Renewal as a Way of Life* is much more than a shorter version of an earlier book. It incorporates seven years of further reflection on the related themes of personal spiritual growth and church renewal. Its special aim is to rebuild Christian spirituality on a stronger foundation: a theology which blends Reformation themes with the biblical teaching on the kingdom of Christ. This approach closely integrates personal spirituality with concerns for church renewal and social transformation.

"The spiritual life" often carries overtones of emotional introspection which give activist Christians claustrophobia. Many are suspicious of piety divorced from concern for public justice. The church is still troubled by the critique of Karl Marx, who said that religion was an opiate for the oppressed and warned against a pietism of the disinherited.

This book aims at a spiritual revolution which will prove Marx wrong. It is designed as an antidote to egocentric spirituality, which flees from the world and neglects the church in a private quest for spiritual perfection. Individual renewal is indissolubly connected to the renewal of the whole church. We cannot attain the fullness of the Spirit without being turned inside out so that our central focus is no longer our own growth, but the glory of God and the growth of Christ's kingdom.

A thoroughly biblical spirituality must attack some unhealthy divisions in Western Christianity: the divorces between spirit and matter, the spiritual and secular realms, clergy and laity. These problems arose when the church became estranged from its Jewish roots. Our anti-Semitism has done more than disfigure our witness. It has also weakened our understanding that Jesus is more than the great High Priest who saves our souls; he is the great King who is to rule and reorder history. I hope that Jewish readers may find that this book describes a Messiah who is worthy of their expectations. It is not Jesus who has failed to satisfy those hopes, but the gentile churches by failing to abide in him. Jewish believers have much to contribute in the continuing inauguration of his reign.

Historically there are two ways of approaching Christian spirituality. One way, which might be called the "ascetic model," emphasizes the cultivation of faith through spiritual disciplines, especially forms of individual prayer and meditation, the broadcasting and receiving cycles of the soul. The other way, which I will call the "charismatic model," stresses that having the Holy Spirit in our lives is a pure gift of God in response to faith, which is another gift. Both models are valid and complementary to one another.

Faith is the main root of spiritual growth. Spiritual disciplines strengthen faith by leading us to prayer and by regularly exposing us to truth, as a solar battery is charged by exposure to light. Taken alone, however, the way of discipline can encourage the delusion that spiritual renewal is a matter of individual achievement. It needs to be balanced by the awareness that we are spiritually renewed as we are refreshed by the gifts of other believers in community and as the Holy Spirit is poured out in answer to corporate prayer. Paul asks, "Did you receive the Spirit by observing the law, or by believing what you heard? . . . After beginning with the Spirit, are you now trying to attain your goal by human effort?" (Gal 3:2-3 NIV).

One or two experiences of the fullness of the Spirit will not produce a fruitful, stable Christian. Therefore this book, which emphasizes faith, could helpfully be studied with another which stresses cultivation, such as Richard Foster's *Celebration of Discipline*. But those whose discipline is weak (or so strong that it tends to obscure dependence on Christ) need to be directed to another word of Paul: "But he said to me, 'My grace is sufficient for you, for my power is made perfect in weakness.' Therefore I will boast all the more gladly about my weaknesses, so that Christ's power may rest on me. . . . For when I am weak, then I am strong" (2 Cor 12:9-10 NIV).

Reading alone, however, is not the most profitable way to use this book. Spiritual growth is not produced by the transfer of information, but by responses of faith. The best way to study *Renewal as a Way of Life* is with a group of persons who are committed, not only to use the discussion questions at the end of each chapter, but also to pray for God to do in their lives and in their churches what is described in the book. These discussion questions also include suggestions for further reading in *Dynamics of Spiritual Life*. I know of several congregations which have been awakened and transformed when a small group of members used *Dynamics* as a focus for revival prayer.

I should make some comments on my use of Scripture in this book. Occasionally I have changed male pronouns or terms so that they are nongender-specific when the reference is inclusive of males and females. For example, "sons" may be changed to "children" when the reference is to all Christians. Also, I have sometimes changed "Christ" to "the Messiah," which is simply substituting the Hebrew term for the Greek. I have done this because I find that most people read "Christ" as Jesus' last name and not as "the anointed king of Israel who will usher in a new kingdom," which is what it actually signifies. For some reason, "Messiah" has not been similarly reduced in meaning and still conveys some of its original majesty.

This work is adapted from a series first presented at Peniel, a renewal center in Lake Luzerne, New York. It incorporates insights from the teaching of Susan Beers, Grover Willcox, Julian Alexander, Malcolm Brown, Bob Henderson, Bill Iverson, Kerry Mumford, Calvin Malefyt, Elward Ellis, Grady Spires, William Brownson and other Peniel leaders. Its structure, like all my work, owes much to the teaching of Donald Mostrom, whose *Intimacy with God* would make a good companion volume.

Part I
The Normal
Christian Life

The God-Centered Life

1

Developing the spiritual life is a growth industry today. Popular religious literature would displace some forms of nonfiction if it were allowed on best-seller lists. Laypeople who have heard about personal commitment to Christ and the fullness of the Holy Spirit on television are urging their pastors to speak on these subjects. Scholars probing the roots of denominations are studying how to recover the spiritual strength of these movements, which began in a blaze of religious experience. Even futurologists, scientists and business leaders are admitting that the moral dilemmas created by technology force us back to religion, both for ethical guidance and for courage to face the future.[1]

In the church, the zealous activism of the 1960s has been overtaken by a new interest in evangelism, worship, prayer and contemplation. Since the Jesus Movement of the late sixties, young converts have been pouring into seminaries, tripling the size of some evangelical schools. The number of Protestant candidates for the ministry is thirty per cent above normal.[2] A study by the Presbyterian Vocation Agency concluded that this is not a threat to the pastoral work force, since past movements of spiritual awakening have always renewed and expanded the church.[3]

The influence of evangelical students and the apparent conservative shift toward Protestant orthodoxy among client congregations have begun to reshape American seminaries. Some leading institutions have begun to hire evangelical faculty, academic deans and presidents. Harvard Divinity School, a bellwether of American intellectual life which has been pointing to the left for almost two hundred years, is now trying to endow a chair of evangelical studies to be occupied by an evangelical scholar.[4] No wonder that *New York Times* religion editor Kenneth Briggs has suggested that the theological leadership of the American church in the late twentieth century, once occupied by Neo-Orthodox figures like Reinhold Niebuhr, is shifting now to progressive evangelicals.[5]

The effect of all this ferment in the life of the church has been no less startling. A recent Presbyterian moderator, Dr. Howard Rice, devoted his moderatorial year to the theme of prayer and spiritual renewal. A zealous activist in the civil rights struggle and other justice issues in the 1960s, Rice had to reorder his priorities when illness halted his movements, put him in a wheelchair and forced him to focus on his relationship with God. In a series of prayer retreats across the country, Rice drew church leaders back into Scripture reading, meditation and prayer. A denominational mission paper reported the results with baffled respect: "Nothing Happened. God Was Worshiped."[6]

Spiritual Self-Centeredness

But this headline has ironic overtones. As we see in Scripture and in past religious awakenings, when God is worshiped, plenty happens! Not only do thousands become converted and spiritually concerned; society is powerfully changed for the better. But while some leaders of the electronic church have become politically active enough to frighten their opponents, most of those involved in the new wave of spiritual interest seem passive and introverted. The *Wall Street Journal* put it this way:

Old Time Religion: An Evangelical Revival is Sweeping the Nation, but with Little Effect.

Millions Quit Mainline Churches for Born-Again Sects that Focus on Inner Self, Shunning the Sinful World

The spirit of religious awakening is once again moving across the land, but unlike a similar great religious awakening two and a half centuries ago that helped sow the seeds of the American Revolution, the current Evangelical revival has so far sowed little except curiosity among unbelievers and self-doubt among many faithful. . . . "I heard on one of those TV evangelism shows that 33% of all Americans are born again," says Douglas Gallagher, pastor of the Bloomfield Baptist Church, near Detroit, and an Evangelical. "But if that is true, why is the crime rate still so high? Why is there still so much use of narcotics? Where is our impact?"

Some of the apparent passivity in the new religious surge may really be constructive action focused on setting one's own house in order. Bill Enright, pastor of the First Presbyterian Church in Glen Ellyn, Illinois, comments in the same *Journal* article: "Two years ago I went on a retreat with the officers from my church and they all said they wanted more sermons that would give them a practical guide on how to live the Christian life in their families, their businesses, their friendships. Too often the church in the past has been esoteric, talking above the people rather than at their level."

But even the conservative revivalists who are said to have influenced the 1980 presidential election have had trouble mobilizing troops for activities outside the church. "Robert Billings, the leader of Moral Majority, says it is difficult to get people steadily involved in anything but their own spiritual lives. 'We get all excited about an issue and go out and organize, and then three weeks later we are back inside the four walls singing "Amazing Grace." ' "[7]

One of my students wrote recently praising Charles Colson's second book, *Life Sentence:*

Colson's realization that the Christian faith goes beyond mere self-improvement . . . proves that spiritual rebirth is not only possible and true but that it is the key to effective social action. . . . I feel that too many evangelicals have become unwitting victims of the societal trademark they so vehemently decry, the "me generation." It seems that they get so wrapped up in this and that course, and that method, tape series, etc., on how to be a better Christian that it becomes the end rather than the means. Their concern seems mostly to center around self, although they hope that their spiritual growth will automatically osmose into those around them.

This is not a new problem. And its presence does not discredit the reality of the religious upsurge. Evangelical awakenings always go through growing pains and spiritual adolescence.[8] John of the Cross, one of the great doctors of Christian spirituality, said that worldly self-interest constantly tries to re-enter the experience of the new convert, masking itself in impressively "spiritual" forms of pride, avarice, envy and gluttony.[9]

But the goal of authentic spirituality is a life which escapes from the closed circle of spiritual self-indulgence, or even self-improvement, to become absorbed in the love of God and other persons. For the essence of spiritual renewal is "the love of God . . . poured out within our hearts through the Holy Spirit" (Rom 5:5 NASB). "My love," said Augustine, "is my weight."[10] The substance of real spirituality is love. It is not our love but God's that moves into our consciousness, warmly affirming that he values and cares for us with infinite concern. But his love also sweeps us away from self-preoccupation into a delight in his unlimited beauty and transcendent glory. It moves us to obey him and leads us to cherish the gifts and graces of others. Paul tells us that love is a far more reliable measure of spirituality than our gifts or works or theological acuity, and that it is one of the few things that last forever (1 Cor 13:8, 13). And Jesus says that the highest fulfillment of the will of God in our lives is to love God with heart and soul and mind and strength, and to care for others as we care for ourselves (Mk 12:30-31).

God at the Center
Self-knowledge and self-fulfillment are considered to be the core of

human achievement by the nonreligious world. The classical Greek counsel was "know thyself." Humanistic psychology and the human potential movement, forces which helped create what Tom Wolfe called "The Me Decade,"[11] have stressed the creative force in each individual which must be set free from society's repressive grip. Yet the search for these goals has produced a lot of people who are at best self-preoccupied and at worst obnoxiously self-assertive.

Religious forms of self-improvement can also generate nervous self-concern and spiritual pride. If growth is built on repressed guilt, or if the means of growth is a set of laws to be followed or an intricate and arduous path to be mastered, spiritual self-centeredness will result.

Biblical self-knowledge and self-fulfillment have their focus outside the self. As John Calvin says, we can only discover ourselves by discovering God. "True and substantial wisdom principally consists of two parts, the knowledge of God, and the knowledge of ourselves. [But] which of them precedes and produces the other, is not easy to discover. [For] no man can take a survey of himself but he must immediately turn to the contemplation of God, in whom he 'lives and moves.' "

But realistic self-examination leads to an awareness of limits, which also drives us to consider God:

Our poverty conduces to a clearer display of the infinite fulness of God. . . . Thus a sense of our ignorance, vanity, poverty, infirmity, depravity, and corruption, leads us to perceive and acknowledge that in the Lord alone are to be found true wisdom, solid strength, perfect goodness, and unspotted righteousness. . . . Nor can we really aspire toward him, till we have begun to be displeased with ourselves. For who would not gladly rest satisfied with himself? Where is the man not absorbed in self-complacency, while he remains unacquainted with his true situation . . . ?[12]

"Feeling good about yourself" is a primary goal of popular psychology, but for biblical religion it is, at best, a way station on the road to knowing God and, at worst, a deceptive trap. Only by fixing our attention on God can we accurately know ourselves—both the graces he has given us and the depth of our needs. If we compare our lives

with those of other human beings, it may be easy for us to say, "I'm
O.K." But if we measure our goodness by the holiness of God, it is
another story.

Encountering the biblical God can be a deeply unsettling experience. The holiness of God is, as Rudolf Otto says, *mysterium tremen-
dum et fascinans*—a tremendous and fascinating mystery.[13] "Hence that
horror and amazement with which the Scripture always represents the
saints to have been impressed and disturbed, on every discovery of
the presence of God."[14] He may be comfortably known and worshiped
at a distance. But a more direct vision of his glory produces holy fear,
an awe not so much of his power as of his purity.

This was Job's experience when God spoke to him out of the whirl-
wind: "My ears had heard of you but now my eyes have seen you.
Therefore I despise myself and repent in dust and ashes" (Job 42:5-
6 NIV). Isaiah reports the same result when he saw the holiness of
God: "Woe is me! For I am lost; for I am a man of unclean lips, and
I dwell in the midst of a people of unclean lips; for my eyes have seen
the King, the LORD of hosts" (Is 6:5).

Even though self-despising is often pathological and self-acceptance is a proper goal of both psychological stability and personal
renewal, the Bible proclaims that self-fulfillment cannot be found
apart from encounter with God. As Johann Tauler put it, "The path-
way to God lies across the track of your own nothingness."[15] Those
who travel that path and find themselves undergoing "the dark night
of the soul," as God purges them from sin in the furnace of conviction, cannot be reassured by easy flattery about their gifts and potential. They may even be discouraged both because no one seems to
understand their condition and because they are being asked to move
too quickly beyond God's purifying work to his peace.

The Fear of the Lord
Awareness of God's holiness and the depth of our sin is the precon-
dition of personal renewal (see figure 1). The experience of God's
people under the Old Covenant is simply schooling in this knowledge.
The mighty acts of God combined with exposure to his law are designed to produce a humble awareness of human sin and divine

goodness. The spiritual goal of the Old Testament is therefore called "the fear of God." "The fear of the LORD is the beginning of wisdom, and the knowledge of the Holy One is understanding" (Prov 9:10 NASB). Spirituality cannot be full or complete unless it is based on faith in Jesus, the Messianic King. But faith in Jesus that is not built on the fear of God, upon a deep hunger and thirst after righteousness, is shallow and fruitless. The shallowness of many people who are "saved" may be due to the fact that they have never known themselves to be lost. Christian spirituality is not complete unless it incorporates the essence of Jewish spirituality.

I. Preconditions of Renewal

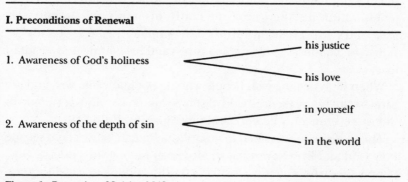

Figure 1: Dynamics of Spiritual Life

God's holiness is his differentness, for the word *holy* means "separate or distinct." God is different from all created beings. We may ask of anything else in reality why it exists, but we cannot ask why God exists. He is the reason for all existence, "the ground of being," as philosophers say. He tells Moses that his name is I AM, the One who is, in a way shared by no other (Ex 3:14).

Part of the differentness of God is his nature. We could not say of any created person, "He is one and at the same time three." But the mystery of God's nature is that individuality and the loving society of the family are both mirrored in his identity. Another way he is unique is that his glory is the goal for which everything else exists: "For from him and through him and to him are all things. To him be the glory forever!" (Rom 11:36 NIV). All intelligent beings are made to worship and serve him, and find their greatest joy and happiness in loving him. God's "jealousy"—his insistence that all other beings must give him supreme praise and honor—would be egoism in any other person. But in him it is simply realism and justice, since he is infinitely worthy of all adoration. All of God's qualities or attributes are different in the same mysterious way. God is not beautiful; he is beauty itself, the fountain from which all beautiful creatures draw their excellence. God is not loving; he is love. His attributes are the infinite standard against which all limited perfections are measured.

Biblical spirituality is based on a deep awareness of all the attributes of God. But there are two of his qualities which are especially important in nurturing "the fear of the Lord": his holy *justice* and his holy *love*. God's self-revelation recorded in Scripture seems especially designed to demonstrate his righteousness and his faithful and steadfast love.

When he is dealing with people who do not know him well and are careless in his presence, God displays his power and grandeur to induce reverence, as he did on Mount Sinai (Ex 19:18-21).

The Israelites understood that no sinful human being could see the holy God and live. Nevertheless, Moses on Mount Sinai asks of God, "I pray thee, show me thy glory" (Ex 33:18). Hidden in a cleft of rock, shielded from God's face and seeing only so much of his glory as humanity can bear, Moses is given a partial revelation of God's nature: "And he passed in front of Moses, proclaiming, 'The LORD, the LORD, the compassionate and gracious God, slow to anger, abounding in love and faithfulness, maintaining love to thousands, and forgiving wickedness, rebellion and sin. Yet he does not leave the guilty unpunished; he punishes the children and their children for the sin of the fathers to the third and fourth generation' " (Ex 34:6-7 NIV).

What is extraordinary about this vision is that even in the context of God's presenting the Law to Moses the primary stress is on God's love. While God makes clear that he cannot be trifled with and will punish the guilty, this is almost an afterthought to declaring his free forgiveness and mercy, his compassion and patience, his faithful and tenacious love. The New Testament, though it takes for granted that God is just, says "God is love," not "God is justice."

God's patience and benevolence are evident too in his dealing with those who are evil. Consider his treatment of the unstable King Ahab, one of the most evil rulers in biblical history (1 Kings 20; see also 21:17-26). An even more depraved king in the southern kingdom, Manasseh, who brought witchcraft into the sanctuary and shed innocent blood, was forgiven when he turned to God in repentance (2 Chron 33:1-20). Even the exile, the great corporate trauma of Israel, is not simply a punishment; it is also a means of purging idolatry from the returning Israelites. Also, in God's wise purpose, those who remain scattered among the nations in the Diaspora form a rail system along which the good news of the Messiah's coming can eventually travel.

The maternal side of God's nature—the impulse which cherishes the potential in children when the paternal impulse of exact justice might disinherit them—is evident in Jesus' lament over the flawed leaders of the Old Covenant: "O Jerusalem, Jerusalem, killing the prophets and stoning those who are sent to you! How often would I have gathered your children together as a hen gathers her brood under her wings, and you would not!" (Mt 23:37; see also the figure of the mother eagle in Deut 32:11).

The Lord of the Old Testament is often thought of as a rigid authoritarian patriarch who demands absolute justice. But the maternal image of patience and mercy is strongly present in the Old Testament portrait of God:

When Israel was a child, I loved him. . . .
It was I who taught Ephraim to walk,
   taking them by the arms;
but they did not realize
   it was I who healed them. . . .
   How can I hand you over, Israel? . . .
My heart is changed within me;
   all my compassion is aroused.
I will not carry out my fierce anger,
   nor will I turn and devastate Ephraim.
For I am God, and not man—
   the Holy One among you. (Hos 11:1, 3, 8-9 NIV)

Even the paternal side of God's nature in the Old Testament is softer than the common image:

The LORD is compassionate and gracious,
Slow to anger and abounding in lovingkindness. . . .
He has not dealt with us according to our sins,
Nor rewarded us according to our iniquities.
For as high as the heavens are above the earth,
So great is His lovingkindness toward those who fear Him. . . .
Just as a father has compassion on his children,
So the LORD has compassion on those who fear him. (Ps 103:8, 10-11, 13 NASB)

The New Testament confirms this portrayal of God's nature in the Messianic acts of Jesus, which are a powerful manifestation of God's desire to heal, bless and restore the fallen creation. Jesus is uniformly patient and merciful with sinners of all kinds, except for the religious leaders who keep multitudes away from God's kingdom by their stubborn pride. In the New Testament as in the Old, God does not wish any to perish (2 Pet 3:9), but "desires all to be saved and to come to the knowledge of the truth" (1 Tim 2:4).

On the other hand, both the Old and New Testaments strongly emphasize the justice of God, his fatherly displeasure with sin in his children, and his holy anger against the rebellion and cruelty of those who are his enemies. The Old Testament revelation of God's nature seems especially calculated to warn callous and insensitive Israelites that they cannot trifle with the One they call Lord. The destruction of Sodom, the Egyptian plagues and the command to destroy the corrupt inhabitants of Canaan are impressive samples of the judicial anger of God, precursors of the Final Judgment. The disciplinary judgments on Israel in the wilderness and the warnings of Deuteronomy 28:15-68, together with their fulfillment in the exile, are examples of his severity in dealing with his own people.

The major and minor prophets produced unsettling documents for young Christians to read, because they seem to alternate between God's gracious promises and scathing outbursts of his anger, like a shower that alternately scalds and cools at chance intervals. These passages are an amazing revelation of the mixed emotions in the heart of God—holy love toward human beings, and holy anger against their destructive sin and injustice.

Human beings have never been eager to hear about God's justice and for the last century American Christians have reacted against the Puritans' enthusiasm for telling them about this side of God's character. Our picture of God has become more and more kindly and humane, like that of an overindulgent grandparent. The portrait of the sovereign God of justice has been dismissed as "Old Testament religion."

But the New Testament just as clearly presents both "the kindness and the severity of God" (Rom 11:22). It begins with an outburst of prophetic warning from John the Baptist (Mt 3:1-12) and Jesus continues to sound this note in his ministry.

The Marcionites in the early church held that Jesus taught a different God from the Lord of the Old Covenant, a kind and friendly God. This heresy has deeply penetrated American Christianity and has almost dissolved its substance. But the biblical Messiah is not the gentle Jesus of Marcion. When he faces unrepentant sin and injustice, he is a commanding figure of prophetic authority.

The Sermon on the Mount, setting forth an ethic of love and humility, which is of transcendent difficulty, warns us, "Unless your righteousness exceeds that of the scribes and Pharisees"—and remember that their spirituality was strenuous and scrupulous—"you will never enter the kingdom of heaven" (Mt 5:20). And this teaching concludes with the warning, "Not every one who says to me, 'Lord, Lord,' shall enter the kingdom of heaven, but he who does the will of my Father" (Mt 7:21).

Jesus' persistent warnings of divine judgment of unrepentant sinners, not merely within time but for eternity, are echoed by all the New Testament writers—even by John, the apostle of love. Although the New Covenant accents God's grace, it retains the Old Testament emphasis on his justice. The letter to the Hebrews makes clear that his character has not changed, and that the clearer disclosure of his grace requires all the more serious obedience to his righteousness: "For we know him who said, 'Vengeance is mine, I will repay.' And again, 'The Lord will judge his people.' It is a fearful thing to fall into the hands of the living God. . . . Strive for peace with all men, and for the holiness without which no one will see the Lord. . . . See that you do not refuse him who is speaking. . . . Let us offer to God acceptable worship, with reverence and awe; for our God is a consuming fire" (Heb 10:30-31; 12:14, 25, 28-29).

New Testament spirituality is still based on the fear of the Lord. Most of us have difficulty nurturing that loving reverence, or respectful love, which is the fear of God. We have been raised by parents who have either spoiled or rejected us, or perhaps have done both. We project their inconsistency and ambivalence on our picture of God. But God is not an arbitrary and authoritarian parent. Love and justice, mercy and anger are not struggling in his nature or flowing and erupting unpredictably. His justice is always controlled and directed by his love. He causes "all things to work together for good to those who love God" (Rom 8:28 NASB). Even sorrow and tragedy are not "accidents," or meaningless evils. They are strokes of discipline his love has designed to conform us more fully to the image of his Son (Phil 3:10; Heb 12:5-11).

Even with his enemies, God's judgment is reluctant. He would have spared Sodom for the sake of a handful of righteous persons. He delayed the invasion of Canaan until the iniquity of its inhabitants was full (Gen 18:32; 15:16). When his justice seems swift and severe, it only abbreviates careers of evil, lessening their ultimate judgment. Sometimes he turns these judgments into beacons to warn against spiritual dangers. When Uzzah is struck dead for reaching out to steady the ark of God (2 Sam 6:6-7), he becomes a warning to David instead of the initiator of a long tradition of irreverence. When Ananias and Sapphira die (Acts 5:1-11), they leave behind them a church sobered into the fear of the Lord, rather than hardened in hypocrisy. God's judgment, as Luther says, is always his "strange work," a work alien to his essential nature of love. But when properly understood it is always consistent with that nature.

The harmony of God's love and justice is perfectly symbolized by the death of Jesus on the cross. The crucifixion reveals the strictness of God's justice in requiring a propitiation for all our sins. But it also shows the depth of his love because he himself offers the required sacrifice. Both the paradox and the harmony of the cross are echoed in the descriptions of Jesus in the book of Revelation. He is both "the Lion of the tribe of Judah," and "the Lamb slain from the foundation of the world" (5:5; 13:8 KJV).

Jesus the Messiah is, as the Puritans understood, "the face of God," the fullest revelation of his love and justice. As we focus on this revelation of God's character, we are spiritually renewed. God increasingly comes to dominate the center of our consciousness. Our minds will turn toward him as automatically as the compass needle seeks the north. We will want our thoughts to be informed by his wisdom until they approximate the mind of Christ. We will want our emotions to respond to events as he responds, and our actions to embody his will.

This is normal and renewed spirituality. But it does not always come easily. The human heart, even the redeemed heart, has an allergy to God. At times we want to avoid God, not only because we want to evade doing his will, but because we retain a slavish fear of him, springing from unbelief.

> Alone, alone, about a dreadful wood
> Of conscious evil runs a lost mankind,
> Dreading to find its Father lest it find
> The Goodness it has dreaded is not good:
> Alone, alone, about our dreadful wood.[16]

I have written at such length about the right kind of fear of God, and the reliability of his love, because there are so many pressures to avoid God hidden in our psychological backgrounds and our fallen human natures.

Love for God
Beyond the presence of a healthy reverence for God and a heart set to imitate his holiness in thought, will and emotional response, there is something more that characterizes fully renewed spirituality: a strong love for God kindled by an inner vision of the heart. Paul prays for the Ephesian Christians to receive this grace:

> that the God of our Lord Jesus Christ, the Father of glory, may give you a spirit of wisdom and of revelation in the knowledge of him, having the eyes of your hearts enlightened, that you may know

> what is the hope to which he has called you, what are the riches
> of his glorious inheritance in the saints, and what is the immeas-
> urable greatness of his power in us who believe, according to the
> working of his great might which he accomplished in Christ when
> he raised him from the dead. (Eph 1:17-20)

This is not an experience which can be worked up by human initiative. It is a gift of sovereign grace, produced by the illuminating
presence of the Spirit of God. This illumination is not given to all
Christians equally, and not every Christian enjoys it continuously. But
since Paul prays that all the Ephesians may receive it, we may assume
that every Christian should experience it in the measure needed to
overcome sin and nourish faith, hope and love. It is because the Holy
Spirit can produce such an illuminated vision of God that he is called
arrabōn, a first installment of heaven itself (Eph 1:14).

There are two theologians who excel in writing about this experience: Jonathan Edwards and Augustine. Edwards, who is mistakenly
associated mainly with dark portrayals of God's judgment, spent most
of his life writing and speaking about the joy of loving God. This
facility came directly from his own experience. In his childhood he
distrusted God's justice. "Absolute sovereignty is what I love to ascribe
to God. But my first conviction was not so." The illuminating work of
the Spirit changed his distrust into love:

> The first instance, that I remember, of that sort of inward, sweet
> delight in God and divine things, that I have lived much in since,
> was on reading of those words, I Tim 1:17: "Now unto the king
> eternal, immortal, invisible, the only wise God, be honour and
> glory for ever and ever." As I read the words, there came into my
> soul, and was as it were diffused through it, a sense of the glory
> of the Divine Being; a new sense, quite different from any thing
> I ever experienced before. I thought within myself, how excellent
> a Being that was, and how happy I should be, if I might enjoy that
> God, and be rapt up to him in heaven; and be as it were swallowed
> up in him for ever![17]

This new apprehension of God's nature included the poles of God's
justice and his love.

I walked abroad alone, in a solitary place in my father's pasture, for contemplation. And as I was walking there, and looking upon the sky and clouds, there came into my mind so sweet a sense of the glorious majesty and grace of God, as I know not how to express. I seemed to see them both in a sweet conjunction; majesty and meekness joined together: it was a sweet, and gentle, and holy majesty; and also a majestic meekness; an awful sweetness; a high, and great, and holy gentleness. . . . The appearance of every thing was altered; there seemed to be, as it were, a calm, sweet cast or appearance of divine glory, in almost every thing. God's excellency, his wisdom, his purity, and love, seemed to appear in every thing: in the sun, moon, and stars; in the clouds and blue sky; in the grass, flowers, trees; in the water and all nature. . . . And scarce any thing, among all the works of nature, was so sweet to me as thunder and lightning; formerly nothing had been so terrible. . . . I had vehement longings of soul after God and Christ, and after more holiness, wherewith my heart seemed to be full, and ready to break. . . . My mind was greatly fixed on divine things; almost perpetually in the contemplation of them. . . . Prayer seemed to be natural to me, as the breath by which the inward burnings of my heart had vent.[18]

It might seem that this measure of spiritual vision would lead to pride. But genuine encounter with God induces humility.

Often . . . I have had very affecting views of my own sinfulness and vileness; very frequently to such a degree, as to hold me in a kind of loud weeping, sometimes for a considerable time together. . . . My wickedness, as I am in myself, has long appeared to me perfectly ineffable, and swallowing up all thought and imagination; like an infinite deluge, or mountains over my head. I know not how to express better what my sins appear to me to be, than by heaping infinite upon infinite, and multiplying infinite by infinite. Very often, for these many years, these expressions are upon infinite— infinite upon infinite! . . . And yet, it seems to me that my conviction of sin is exceedingly small and faint.[19]

Having experienced an ennobling and humbling vision of the divine glory, Edwards was able to speak of this in his sermons. When during the Great Awakening the townspeople of Northampton went through their collective dark night of the soul, gripped by deep conviction of sin and lifted to similar perceptions of the excellency of God and Christ, Edwards was able to counsel his people and describe their experience accurately. His description of his wife's experience during the Awakening suggests a paradigm of the God-centered life. He records that she had

> an extra ordinary sense of the awful majesty, greatness, and holiness of God . . . a sense of the glorious, unsearchable, unerring wisdom of God in his works . . . a sweet rejoicing of soul at the thoughts of God being infinitely and unchangeably happy, and an exulting gladness of heart that God is self-sufficient, and infinitely above all dependence, and reigns over all, and does his will with absolute and uncontrollable power and sovereignty [and with] a universal benevolence to mankind, with a longing as it were to embrace the whole world in the arms of pity and love. [She had] a vehement and constant desire for the setting up of Christ's kingdom through the earth, as a kingdom of holiness, purity, love, peace, and happiness to mankind. . . . The strength was very often taken away with longings that others might love God more, and serve God better, and have more of his comfortable presence . . . a compassionate grief towards fellow-creatures—a daily sensible doing and suffering every thing for God . . . eating, working, sleeping, and bearing pain and trouble for God, and doing all as the service of love, with a continual uninterrupted cheerfulness, peace, and joy. Oh how good . . . is it to work for God in the day-time, and at night to lie down under his smiles![20]

The Great Awakening motivated an explosion of activity which remade American society and led to the birth of a new nation infused with Christian principles. But there were deep roots to this activity which are often lacking in modern activism, both among "evangelicals and socially concerned "liberals." Much religious life in the twentieth century seems to lose track of the one who is supposedly at its center: God.

In contrast, Augustine, the foundational theologian of Christianity, was relentlessly God-centered. Like Edwards, Augustine recognized that human action is motivated by desire, by love. "The whole life of a good Christian is a holy desire,"[21] that is, a desire for God. "Thou hast made us for thyself, O Lord, and our hearts are restless till they rest in thee."[22]

But the life that is not centered on God is also driven by desire, by a displaced love centered on lesser goods. "Late have I loved Thee, O Beauty so ancient and so new, late have I loved Thee! . . . I was looking for Thee out there, and I threw myself, deformed as I was, upon those well-formed things which Thou hast made. . . . These things held me far from Thee, things which would not have existed had they not been in Thee. Thou didst call and cry out and burst in upon my deafness; Thou didst shine forth and glow and drive away my blindness; Thou didst send forth Thy fragrance, and I drew in my breath, and now I pant for Thee; I have tasted, and now I hunger and thirst; Thou didst touch me, and I was inflamed with desire for Thy peace."[23]

In the 1960s, God became so peripheral to much religious activity that it came as no surprise when some theologians announced that he was dead. Religious social activism not rooted in love for God is driven by love for idols. It pretends to come from concern for others or for God's kingdom, but actually it is motivated by the worship of humanity or disguised forms of self-glorification.

On the other hand, evangelical religion as an aid to self-assurance, health or wealth really short-circuits the soul's path toward contact with God, which is the heart's deepest desire. As Augustine observes, "Many cry to the Lord to avoid losses or to acquire riches, for the safety of their friends or the security of their homes, for temporal felicity or worldly distinction, yes, even for mere physical health which is the sole inheritance of the poor man. . . . Alas, it is easy to want things from God and not to want God himself; as though the gift could ever be preferable to the giver."[24] Or, as he says elsewhere, "The soul cannot rest save in that which it loves. But eternal rest is given to it only in the love of God, who alone is eternal."[25]

Augustine's spirituality is not based on the denigration of material things. He is not asking us to turn from these to a separate, "spiritual" realm. He takes seriously the fact that everything God has created is good and that the beauty of creation legitimately and powerfully attracts our love. But we cannot fully appreciate created goods unless

our deepest love is fixed on the Good behind them. We are to use
created beauty as a ladder to climb to the Creator:

> God does not forbid the love of these things but only the finding
> of our happiness in the love of them. We should make the love of
> their Creator the end of our esteem for them. Suppose, brethren,
> a man should make a ring for his betrothed, and she should love
> the ring more than her betrothed, would not her heart be convict-
> ed of infidelity? . . . God, then, has given you all things: love him
> who made them.[26]

> Leave, then, all other desires. He who made heaven and earth
> is more beautiful than all things. . . . Learn, then, to love the Crea-
> tor in the creature. . . . Never permit what was made by him to take
> such a hold upon you that you lose him by whom you yourself were
> made.[27]

Augustine is deeply aware that we are moving through a damaged
creation, where the good gifts of God stir up in our hearts inordinate
affection, which makes our love for God intermittent. And so he reminds us that we are moving toward a different state of being in which
God will perpetually remain at the center of our love and experience.
We are moving toward "the everlasting reign of those who perfectly
praise him because they perfectly love him; who perfectly love him
because they see him face to face."[28] "One thing I have asked of the
Lord. What shall we do in that home in which we hope to dwell all
the days of our lives? Listen: 'That I may contemplate the beauty of
the Lord.' . . . What a glorious vision will be presented to us in the
contemplation of the beauty of the Lord!"[29]

> There we shall rest and we shall see; we shall see and we shall love;
> we shall love and we shall praise.[30]

> For when, after these labours, we come to that rest, the praise
> of God will be our sole occupation. Our activity there will be "Al-
> leluia" . . . our food will be "Alleluia"—the praise of God.[31]

> Today, hope sings it, and sometimes love. But then love alone
> shall sing it. The love that sometimes sings it in this life is a love
> of desire; whereas it will then be sung by a love that rejoices in the
> everlasting possession of its beloved.[32]

> There shall peace be made perfect in the sons of God, all loving

one another, seeing one another possessed of God, since God shall be all in all. We shall be all in all. We shall have God as our common vision, God as our common possession, God as our common peace. And whatever there is that he gives us here and now, he himself will be in place of all his gifts. He will be our full and perfect peace. . . . Our peace, our rest, our joy, the end of all our troubles, is none but God.[33]

Our present troubled existence is only a brief, rapid, dreamlike prelude to an eternity which we will spend in a direct relationship with God and others, unhindered by sin. "What I mean, brothers, is that the time is short. . . . For this world in its present form is passing away" (1 Cor 7:29, 31 NIV).

We do not know much about the kind of life we will enjoy in eternity. But we do know that God will be at the center of the kingdom of heaven. We read in Revelation 4 that God will sit upon his throne, surrounded by twenty-four thrones representing the leaders of the Old and New Covenants, and by innumerable living beings absorbed in worship. The greatest blessing of the City of God will be unhindered fellowship with him: "The throne of God and of the Lamb will be in the city, and his servants will serve him. They will see his face" (Rev 22:3-4 NIV). What is impossible now will be realized then: the vision of the face of God.

The God-centered life is spirituality as it is meant to be. It is how we were made to live. It is how we will soon be living for eternity, freed from all our present inward restraints. If God is the central reality of our lives, and if our main purpose in living is "to glorify Him and to enjoy Him for ever,"[34] then it is only realistic for us to live our lives increasingly with God at the center.

Discussion Questions

Recommended supplemental reading: Preface to my *Dynamics of Spiritual Life* (IVP). Scripture for meditation: Exodus 33:1-23; 34:1-9.

1. Do you think a new spiritual awakening is occurring now? What signs of this do you see?

2. What weaknesses do you see in today's spirituality?

3. What symptoms of self-centeredness rather than God-centeredness can you identify in religious life today?

4. What does the phrase "the fear of the Lord" suggest to you? Is this a good description for Christian spirituality? Do we need this quality today?

5. When have you been most aware of loving God?

6. What problems do you encounter in loving God and keeping him at the center of your life?

7. How important is the experience of worshiping God in your personal life? in your church?

The Kingdom-Centered Life 2

The foundation of both Jewish and Christian spirituality is the Shema: "Hear, O Israel: The LORD our God is one LORD; and you shall love the LORD your God with all your heart, and with all your soul, and with all your might" (Deut 6:4-5). When Jesus was asked to identify the great commandment of the Law, he quoted this passage, adding a quotation from the Torah (Lev 19:18): "This is the great and first commandment. And a second is like it, You shall love your neighbor as yourself. On these two commandments depend all the law and the prophets" (Mt 22:38-40).

In saying that the command to love our neighbors as ourselves is like the command to love God, Jesus may mean that it is of similar importance in human conduct. (After all, directions about interpersonal relationships make up more than half the Ten Commandments.) Or he may mean that we can only love and obey God wholeheartedly when we love our neighbors as we do ourselves. In any case, the love of others is vital to a fully developed spiritual life.

Jesus takes for granted a truth which modern psychologists have rediscovered: that in order to love others properly, we must first love ourselves. Just as we have a powerful drive to love which cannot be satisfied until it finds God, we also have a deep hunger to be loved, to experience the affirmation of our gifts and value as persons. Only when we have this affirmation can we love ourselves. Our hearts are restless until they find their rest in God, but they are also ill at ease without a sense of our dignity as corulers of creation. Only by seeing our mirrored reflection as we look at God do we have a proper self-love, and are then freed to truly love others.

Those out of contact with God are forced to find their sense of value and identity elsewhere. They must get a black market substitute for God's love from psychiatrists or other human beings. But this need for love and dignity is so great that self-admiration and the love of others cannot begin to satisfy it. We can cheer ourselves up only so long by repeating the pitiful fiction "I'm O.K.—You're OK." Then we begin to check our own credentials, and our therapist's, for making such judgments.

Secular psychologists may respond that Christians like Augustine and Edwards promote an unhealthy and negative self-concept—what might be called a "guilty worm" neurosis. Unfortunately, many Christians do try to live with a bad self-image, mistaking it for the virtue of humility. But this is the devil's estimate of their character and gifts. Humiliation does not produce humility; instead, it creates an open psychological wound that inhibits our ability to love ourselves, God and others. The Bible does not advise us to think ill of ourselves, only to think realistically: "Do not think of yourself more highly than you ought, but rather think of yourself with sober judgment, in accordance with the measure of faith God has given you" (Rom 12:3 NIV).

Realistic self-affirmation is perfectly compatible with deep conviction of sin. Jonathan Edwards was certainly aware of his gifts and graces. He displays no false humility. But he was aware of the responsibility that those gifts entailed, and the damage they could do apart from the Spirit's control. Redemption has made us kings. But in this life the head that wears a crown will often rest uneasy because of responsibilities and failures.

In the Great Awakening the outpouring the the Holy Spirit produced not only an illuminated vision of God, but also a passionate concern for other human beings. This is quite natural. For we cannot love God unless through the Spirit's work we are swept into the flow of his love as it moves through us and back to himself. And as it moves through us it flows outward also to embrace his creation. The same love that binds us to God binds us to our neighbor. True spirituality cannot divorce the one from the other.

We must be wary of forms of spirituality which concentrate on God or the spiritual realm at the expense of humanity and society. Eastern mysticism and Western asceticism commonly make this error. The problem with this outlook is well symbolized by a text from the German poet Ruckert, set in a lovely song by Gustav Mahler: "I have become lost to the world, with which I once spent so much time. . . . I am dead to worldly tumult, and rest in a realm of calm. I live alone, in my heaven, in my love, in my song." This sort of spirituality is vulnerable to the charge that it is a "pietism of the disinherited"—an opiate taken to kill the pain of failure or material poverty, or, even worse, given by economic oppressors for that purpose. Spirituality which neglects the love of neighbor, and which fails to seek justice for the neighbor, is simply not biblical.

God's Kingdom and the Love of Neighbors

But who is my neighbor? This question evoked a famous response from Jesus: the parable of the good Samaritan (Lk 10:29-37). His point was that anybody I come in contact with who is in need is my neighbor, including those who might normally be my enemies. God's love flows through us, enabling us not only to appreciate the gifts and excellencies of all persons, but also to bless and help those near us, even when they hate us.

Loving others, then, is not simply good behavior according to God's rules. It is imitating his love by participating in his loving outreach toward the needy, including his enemies and ours. Jesus makes this plain: "You have heard that it was said, 'You shall love your neighbor and hate your enemy.' But I say to you, Love your enemies and pray for those who persecute you, so that you may be children of your Father who is in heaven; for he makes his sun rise on the evil and on the good, and sends rain on the just and on the unjust" (Mt 5:43-45). The whole fabric of nature is organized as a means of care and a message of God's love for fallen humanity. Believers are to become part of this system of care and communication, as they are indwelt by the Holy Spirit and express his love toward others.

But nature has been distorted by the Fall, and delivers an ambivalent message to unbelievers. Nature gives them enough joy and satisfaction to point them toward a benevolent Creator, but it also provides enough crises and disasters to encourage them to seek God. God insists on giving us what we need rather than what we want. And what we need, according to John's Revelation, is something like a continuous replay of the ten plagues of Egypt! (It is hard to discern why some disasters seem to fall on the wrong persons. But Jesus observes that the more sensible question is why they do not fall on us all because of our sins [Lk 13:1-5].)

God's people, however, convey a less ambiguous message of love and care for humanity. In our lives we can express a pure message of love, mercy and concern from the heart of God. We can help heal the wounds inflicted by spiritual warfare. When confronted with the plagues of nature, we can point to a God who uses them to facilitate deliverance, to push us to repent of our sins and call on God for salvation.

And we can redistribute material blessings to help the materially poor. Both spiritual and material goods tend to accumulate in an unbalanced way. God's material blessings sometimes visibly fall upon believers, commending faith to those who are outside. But Christians can be arms of God's love reaching out to redistribute material wealth, and hence commend the gospel to the poor, sharing spiritual wealth. A less exalted reason for the uneven distribution of material wealth is human avarice. In this case, Christians can often design or support initiatives which overcome some of the inequities resulting from policies that let the rich get richer and the poor get poorer.

The meaning of this enterprise is deepened by Jesus' explanation that those involved are really ministering to him: "Then the King will say to those at his right hand, 'Come, O blessed of my Father, inherit the kingdom prepared for you from the foundation of the world; for I was hungry and you gave me food, I was thirsty and you gave me drink, I was a stranger and you welcomed me, I was naked and you clothed me, I was sick and you visited me, I was in prison and you came to me' " (Mt 25:34-36). Every person in need may turn out to be a member of the body of Christ. And so there is a sense in which care for our neighbors is just another expression of our love for God.

The love of neighbors, then, is far more extensive than it first appears to be. In this century international telecasts make us neighbors of all the wretched of the earth. As Pope John Paul II said during one of his American visits, we in the Western world are the rich man, and much of the rest of the world is Lazarus at our gate (Lk 16:19-31). We are responsible to care for the needs of those near us in our homes and communities. But we should also be involved in an enterprise of spiritual and physical care which spans the nations.

At this point, something within us may be protesting, "That's too much responsibility! God allows famines and earthquakes. Why should I have to take up the slack? Whole nations are shutting out the gospel and getting plagues to awaken them. Why do I have to come up with the means to evangelize them?"

Our answer lies in Jesus' teaching about prayer in the parable of the reluctant neighbor (Lk 11:5-8). This story is about a person who needs food for a visitor, and so wakes up a friend at midnight to ask for bread. "I tell you, though he will not get up and give him the bread because he is his friend, yet because of the man's persistence he will get up and give him as much as he needs. So I say unto you: Ask and it will be given to you; seek and you will find; knock and the door will be opened to you. For everyone who asks receives; he who seeks finds; and to him who knocks, the door will be opened" (Lk 11:8-10 NIV). This promise is usually applied to petitions for our own needs, but the context involves gaining resources *for others*. Jesus goes on to say that God, far from being a sleepy neighbor, is eager to bless his children: "Which of you fathers, if your son asks for a fish, will give him a snake instead? . . . If you then, though you are evil, know how to give good gifts to your children, how much more will your Father in heaven give the Holy Spirit to those who ask him!" (Lk 11:11, 13 NIV).

This parable comes right after Luke's presentation of the Lord's Prayer (Lk 11:2-4). It is important to recognize that the Lord's Prayer combines petitions for our own needs and intercession for others under a single category: the coming of the kingdom of the Messiah. When we pray "thy kingdom come, thy will be done, on earth as it is in heaven" (the fuller version from Mt 6:10), we are essentially asking that the reign of God will advance in our lives and those of our neighbors throughout the world.

Love for our neighbors, then, like love for ourselves, involves something vastly more significant than the meeting of individual needs. It involves God's reaching out in us and through us to build a kingdom, a sphere of rulership, in which his will is done in the fallen world as it is in the sinless heavens; in which cruelty and disorder and the distortion caused by sin are supplanted by love, order and righteousness. Loving obedience to God produces much more than individual goodness, respectability and the alleviation of suffering. It builds the kingdom of heaven.

Old Testament Images of the Messianic Kingdom

If loving ourselves and loving our neighbors as ourselves are really best understood as promoting the reign of God, then biblical spirituality is intimately connected with God's kingdom. But the kingdom of God is not something we hear much about today. We hear a great deal about the church and the Christian life and, in some churches, about social needs. But seldom do we hear about God's kingdom in connection with these. Yet when we read the Bible, the kingdom of God is the central theme which ties together everything, both in the Old Testament and in the New.

There is a reason for this. One of the ruling passions of humanity is the search for a righteous government. The poor and the disadvantaged contend against "the system" with the conviction that another economic order will make the world livable. Every four years the American people elect a new president with the hope that somehow this will make things better. Economic downturns, crop failures, moral declines and worsening international conditions are all blamed on presidents—who in most cases have little control over events. In the hearts of the people is a groping, inarticulate conviction that if the right ruler would only come along, the world would be healed of all its wounds. Creation is headless and desperately searching for its head.

This search is the "plot" of the Old and New Testaments. Genesis begins with man and woman rejecting the rule of God in order to exercise their own rule. The effect of this revolt is to make human beings puppet kings, clinging to the illusion of independent control while actually enslaved by their own passions and by darker spiritual forces. The Garden becomes the Wasteland. Thebes withers under the rule of Oedipus, the guilty king who has forgotten his terrible sin. Human evil and demonic violence rack and torment the world so that even inanimate nature cries out for deliverance (Rom 8:19-23). "The dark places of the earth are full of the habitations of cruelty" (Ps 74:20 KJV). The kingdom which was made to be ruled by man and woman in partnership with God laments because man has brought it under a curse; it longs for a new ruler.

The "good news" is that by God's undeserved kindness this ruler has been promised and that he has come. God tells the serpent, "I will put enmity between you and the woman, and between your offspring and hers; he will crush your head, and you will strike his heel" (Gen 3:15 NIV). What is promised is a stricken king, a wounded healer, who will tread underfoot the works of darkness and subject the earth once more to the rule of God and man, displacing the invading powers.

This coming ruler, the Messiah, is promised as the seed of Abraham. Although all nations are to be blessed through Abraham's literal descendants, it is particularly through one of his offspring that all ethnic groups are to enter the fullness of blessing, the Messianic kingdom. Left to themselves, these different nations become rival gangs whose corporate selfishness drives them to neglect one another in peace or afflict one another in war. They can find blessing for themselves and concord with one another only as they submit themselves to the Messiah and their leaders yield to his direction.

The Old Testament gives no hint that all this is to be true only in a spiritual realm beyond history. Ordinary experience is to be hallowed through the promised Messiah. Even the divinely ordered architecture of the Jewish tabernacle, which the letter to the Hebrews calls "a copy and shadow of what is in heaven," speaks symbolically not of ethereal spiritual realities, but of the kingdom of God on earth. As Franz Delitzsch comments:

> In the symbolism of antiquity, the square was a symbol of the universe or cosmos . . . a type of the world as the scene of divine revelation, the sphere of the kingdom of God, for which the world from the very first had been intended. . . . Hence the seal of the kingdom of God was impressed upon the sanctuary . . . through the quadrangular form that was given to its separate rooms. . . . The direction in which it was set up, towards the four quarters of the heavens, showed that the kingdom of God that was planted in Israel was intended to embrace the entire world, while the oblong shape given to the whole building set forth the idea of the present incompleteness of the kingdom, and the cubic form of the most holy place, its ideal and ultimate perfection.[1]

"The heavenly things" were not divorced from present realities as can also be seen in the Messianic sacrifice. What took place in the atonement was the hallowing of life, through the resurrection of a new humanity and the inauguration of the kingdom of God on earth.

On the other hand, the inception of the kingdom involves an invasion of spiritual and supernatural reality into ordinary existence. Under the Old Covenant, Israel treasured the tablets of the Law in the ark of the covenant, the sacred box within the holy of holies. The ark was a talisman which was carried about at the head of Israel's armies to establish or defend her kingdom. But under the New Covenant, biblical revelation is no longer to be carried in boxes, but is written on the hearts of God's people as they move about establishing or preserving the kingdom of God. The cherishing of the written Word of God, which the Holy Spirit illumines for those who have faith in the incarnate Word of God, brings the atmosphere of heaven to every part of life.

In the Old Testament, God warns Israel that most human kings will not hallow life, but will turn it into building materials for the Tower of Babel.

> This is what the king who will reign over you will do: He will take your sons and make them serve with his chariots and horses, and they will run in front of his chariots. Some he will assign to be commanders of thousands and commanders of fifties, and others to plow his ground and reap his harvest, and still others to make weapons of war and equipment for his chariots. He will take your daughters to be perfumers and cooks and bakers. . . . He will take a tenth of your grain and of your vintage and give it to his officials and attendants. . . . He will take a tenth of your flocks, and you yourselves will become his slaves. When that day comes, you will cry out for relief from the king you have chosen, and the LORD will not answer you in that day. (1 Sam 8:11-18 NIV)

Things have not changed since biblical times. Building Babel is still an expensive business.

And so the earthly Israelite kingdom is at its worst a devastating failure. At best, in David's reign and certain features of Solomon's, it is another "copy and shadow" of better things to come in the Messianic kingdom. When David has established his own kingdom and proposes to build a permanent dwelling for God in the form of a temple, God reminds him that he has never requested a cedar house to live in. Then he says, "I declare to you that the LORD will build a house for you. . . . I will raise up . . . one of your own sons, and I will establish his kingdom. He is the one who will build a house for me." The prophecy appears at first to refer only to Solomon, who did build the first temple. But it goes on to say, "I will set him over my house and my kingdom forever; his throne will be established forever" (1 Chron 17:10-12, 14 NIV). Obviously the ultimate reference is to the Messiah, who built the final house of God through his life, death and resurrection. Jesus established the kingdom of God through the incorporation of believers in his body to be priests and kings within a temple built of living stones. Thus the original intent of creation—that man and God should rule as partners over the creatures—is accomplished in a way too marvelous to hope for: God and man united in one person, the pioneer and perfecter of a human kingdom pervaded by the Holy Spirit.

The kingdom of the God-man is to begin in ordinary history and never cease growing.

> For to us a child is born,
> to us a son is given;
> and the government will be upon his shoulder,
> and his name will be called
> "Wonderful Counselor, Mighty God,
> Everlasting Father, Prince of Peace."
> Of the increase of his government and of peace
> there will be no end. (Is 9:6-7)

In the midst of recurring conflicts between the nations—represented in Daniel's apocalyptic visions as segments of a human statue or great beasts conquering one another in succession—the Son of man is presented before the Ancient of Days, and is given "dominion and glory and kingdom, that all peoples, nations, and languages should serve him . . . an everlasting dominion, which shall not pass away . . . one that shall not be destroyed." His rule will be shared by the people of God, for "the greatness of the kingdoms under the whole heaven shall be given to the people of the saints of the Most High; their kingdom shall be an everlasting kingdom, and all dominions shall serve and obey them" (Dan 7:14, 27).

The Messiah's conquest of the nations is presented in Daniel 2 in the vision of a stone cut by no human hand. This stone strikes the feet of mixed clay and iron in the human idol and smashes them—the feet represent the third in the succession of great kingdoms following the Babylonian rule, evidently the unstable amalgam of the Roman Empire. And, as Daniel says, "In the days of those kings the God of heaven will set up a kingdom which shall never be destroyed, nor shall its sovereignty be left to another people. It shall break in pieces all these kingdoms and bring them to an end, and it shall stand for ever" (Dan 2:44). The stone, which typifies both the Messiah and his followers, first strikes the image, and then it becomes a great mountain which fills the whole earth. This vision is reminiscent of the second chapter of Isaiah:

In the last days
the mountain of the LORD's temple will be established
   as chief among the mountains;
it will be raised above the hills,
   and all nations will stream to it.
Many peoples will come and say,
   "Come, let us go up to the mountain of the LORD,
   to the house of the God of Jacob.
He will teach us his ways,
   so that we may walk in his paths."
The law will go out from Zion,
   the word of the LORD from Jerusalem.
He will judge between the nations
   and will settle disputes for many peoples.
They will beat their swords into plowshares
   and their spears into pruning hooks.
Nation will not take up sword against nation,
   nor will they train for war anymore. (Is 2:2-4 NIV)

This prophecy speaks not of the destruction and judgment of the adversary nations, but of their subjection and transformation through the influence of the Messiah and his people. It holds out a promise of peace which seems almost too good to be true in ordinary history, especially in the present time of fear and despair over the nuclear arms race. But it seems to say that the nations are to be transformed through the discipling impact of the word of God. The temple here might typify the glorified body of the risen Lord. But it is more likely that it reaches to include the body of Christ within history.

On the other hand, the image of "the mountain of the Lord" in Isaiah and other prophets blends inevitably into the final peace of the eternal state: "On this mountain the LORD of hosts will make for all peoples a feast of fat things, a feast of wine on the lees, of fat things full of marrow, of wine on the lees well refined. And he will destroy on this mountain the covering that is cast over all peoples, the veil that is spread over all nations. He will swallow up death for ever, and the Lord GOD will wipe away tears from all faces" (Is 25:6-8).

It is hard to tell how much of this is possible before the New

Jerusalem descends from heaven, bringing "new heavens and a new earth in which righteousness dwells" (2 Pet 3:13). But it is clear that "the increase of his government and of peace" is not a quantum jump from a long period of negligible control among the nations to an instant harmony brought about by the return of Christ. Rather it is a steady growth in which the stone cut without hands becomes a mountain.

This is clearly the meaning of another Old Testament image of the progress of Christ's kingdom. Ezekiel sees a vision of a second temple with a stream of water flowing from the altar. At first it is shallow and narrow, but as it flows, it constantly broadens and deepens, until it is so large no one can cross. Wherever it goes life springs up, salt water is turned to fresh, and even the Dead Sea becomes an oasis of vitality. This is evidently a picture of the increasing growth and influence of the kingdom of God within history.

New Testament Images of the Kingdom of God

After the failure of the theocracy, the prophets pointed more and more to the coming reign of God, when his prince, the Messiah, would overcome and punish all enemies. The Messiah would restore his people in righteousness, in healing, in a world set free from the primeval curse to become a universal and eternal Eden (for example, see Is 11:6-9).

The Gospels record the good news of the Messiah's coming. Understandably, they present the kingdom of God (also called "the kingdom of heaven") as the organizing theme of Jesus' preaching. Jesus begins his ministry by proclaiming, "The time is fulfilled, and the kingdom of God is at hand; repent and believe in the gospel" (Mk 1:15 NASB). Jesus' preaching is much more centered on the kingdom, and the way of life consistent with it, than most current sermons, although he does continually stress the need for faith in his own power and authority. The same is true of the preaching of the apostles in Acts. The message that brings salvation to those that believe is that Jesus is the Messiah, the anointed king of Israel, and that he has been raised from the dead.

The connection between "the good news" and the kingdom of God is obscured for Christians by the use of the Greek word *Christ* for Messiah throughout our translations of the New Testament. Every time we come across the phrase "Jesus Christ," instead of hearing "Jesus, the king who was promised to Israel," all we hear is "Jesus" followed by a meaningless syllable. For most, probably, the phrase means "Jesus, who saves me from my sins." This is certainly true, but it falls far short of saying "Jesus, the ruler of a whole new order of life, who has delivered me so that I can be part of it."

Although Scripture clearly teaches that with Jesus' death and resurrection the battle against the occupying world powers has been decisively won (Col 2:15; Jn 12:31; 2 Cor 2:14; Heb 2:14), the results of this have to be worked out in history. There is a continuing war of liberation through which multitudes, both Jews and Gentiles, will submit themselves to the king. In David's case there was an interval between his anointing by Samuel and the time when the tribes, freed from the bad leadership of Saul, united under his reign. Something similar is occurring now. This is not a time for rest and relaxation and the uninterrupted enjoyment of spiritual peace. While on earth, we are in a spiritual battle, although happily our tour of duty is limited and soon leads to eternal rest. It is not a time for single-minded concentration on getting and spending, "eating and drinking, marrying and giving in marriage" (Mt 24:38). The war for the establishment of the kingdom creates a continual state of emergency which has a priority above these necessary and enjoyable activities (Acts 14:22). Jesus' marching orders are, "Seek first his kingdom and his righteousness, and all these things shall be yours as well" (Mt 6:33).

And yet for believers every normal activity is a part of kingdom warfare. For the kingdom of God is nothing other than the proper ordering of all our activities within the framework of obedient love of God and compassionate love of neighbors. The most crucial battle for the kingdom is won every time a human being repents, believes and submits to the lordship of the Messiah, becoming a new center for the reordering of life on earth as it is in heaven. Repentance (*metanoia*, having a new mind about God, ourselves and others) is the most dynamic inrush of the kingdom within ordinary history. When we repent we enter the kingdom, and the kingdom enters history in a little larger measure (Mk 9:47; Lk 18:16; Jn 3:3).

This is the point of Jesus' parables of the kingdom in Matthew 13. "The word of the kingdom" (13:19) takes root in individual hearts and begins a transforming process which bears fruit. Such individuals are like the grain in a field, or the fish in a net, which must not be prematurely separated from weeds or inedible fish because this would arrest the growth of the kingdom (13:36-43, 47-50). That growth is quiet and almost imperceptible, "like leaven which a woman took and hid in three measures of flour, till it was all leavened" (13:33). "The kingdom of heaven is like a grain of mustard seed . . . the smallest of all seeds, but when it has grown it is the greatest of shrubs and becomes a tree, so that the birds of the air come and make nests in its branches" (13:31-32; see also Ezek 17:22-24).

This concept of the gradual appearance of the kingdom proved frustrating to the Jewish leaders in Jesus' time. Asked by the Pharisees when the kingdom was coming, Jesus replied, "The kingdom of God is not coming with signs to be observed; nor will they say, 'Lo, here it is!' or 'There!' for behold, the kingdom of God is in the midst of you" (Lk 17:20-21). As Paul observed, while Gentiles were preoccupied with a search for religious wisdom, the more down-to-earth Jews were looking for "signs," miraculous breakthroughs which would provide them with the benefits of the kingdom here and now. "But we preach the Messiah crucified, a stumbling block to Jews and folly to Gentiles, but to those who are called, both Jews and Greeks, the Messiah the power of God and the wisdom of God" (1 Cor 1:23-24).

And yet modern Jews and other realists have a point when they shrug and comment, "The Messiah has come? So what's different?" Yeast is quiet and gradual in its operation. But if it is alive, it always gets the job done in fairly short order. Jesus said, "You are the salt of the earth" (Mt 5:13). Salt which has not lost its potency inhibits corruption. Yet nominally Christian countries, which ought to be gardens of Messianic transformation, are jungles of corruption. Lives in which the power of the kingdom is really working ought to be extensions of Messianic authority and power. Heaven's order ought to be flowing into the earth around them. Jesus promised the disciples, "He who believes in me will also do the works that I do; and greater works than these will he do. . . . Whatever you ask in my name, I will do it" (Jn 14:12-13). The Messiah's rule is to be implemented by Messianic believers.

The full stature of the community of believers is indicated in 1 Peter 2:4-10. Messianic people exercise the same offices as the Messiah toward those around them. They are "a holy priesthood, to offer spiritual sacrifices acceptable to God through Jesus the Messiah" (2:5). They are not only priests, but also kings and prophets: "a chosen race, a royal priesthood, a holy nation, God's own people, that you may declare the wonderful deeds of him who called you out of darkness into his marvelous light" (1 Pet 2:9). Through them the Messiah continues to expand his reign on earth. Through them he reconciles others to God, says what needs to be said to the nations in prophetic criticism, and subjects rebellious persons and systems to his rule.

To fulfill this role is not an onerous task but a glorious privilege. Jesus compares participation in the kingdom to a "treasure hidden in a field, which a man found and covered up; then in his joy he goes and sells all that he has and buys that field. Again, the kingdom of heaven is like a merchant in search of fine pearls, who, on finding one pearl of great value, went and sold all that he had and bought it" (Mt 13:44-46). The exercise of "the powers of the age to come" (Heb 6:5) in kingdom-centered lives is worth the subordination of all other enterprises.

The Messianic Kingdom and the Gentile Church

During most of its existence, however, the church has had a tenuous hold on the idea of the kingdom of God. The early church concentrated on the kingdom, but only to hope for a quick end to persecution. Ironically, it was during this period that Christians conquered the Roman Empire for Christ! Their witness penetrated every class from the slaves through the nobility, until a Christian emperor became a live option. In this unexpected situation, Christians were able to begin reshaping the pagan social environment, to make it subject to the Messiah.

Augustine responded to this new situation by shifting the Christian understanding of history. He turned the church away from passive waiting for the Messiah's return and urged an increasingly aggressive missionary outreach, a continued spiritual warfare to expand the rule of Christ among pagans. But other elements of his thought undercut this kingdom emphasis. In the Donatist controversy, he decided that the kingdom must be forced on dissidents by the arm of the civil magistrate: "Compel them to come in." In the hands of the Inquisition and the Reformers, this coercive strategy consistently failed to eliminate heresy and generated secular humanist responses like the Italian Renaissance and the Enlightenment. Augustine's helpful distinction between the City of God and the City of man failed to recognize that the church has too much residual sin to allow it to put a straitjacket on the world, while the world, through God's common grace, contains truth and creativity often neglected by the church.

Although Augustine rejected the Manichaean extreme which teaches that the material creation is evil, his thought remains tinged with the Greek dualism between spirit and matter. The Neo-Platonic influence in his theology can draw Christians into the glowing world of ideas, while the ordinary world of human endeavor goes to ruin. Medieval Christianity turned healthy, earthy Jewish piety, with its concern for responsible living in the here and now, into an otherworldly hope centered on "pie in the sky when you die," as Marxist critics would say.

Augustine's conversion to monastic asceticism added an ideal of moral heroism which put spiritual renewal beyond the reach of ordinary laypeople. Among the clergy, the ascetic version of "the deeper Christian life" did not heal and transform our strongest areas of bondage—the pursuit of wealth, power and sensual gratification. Instead, they simply amputated these areas of human experience through the monastic sanctification machine, with its vows of poverty, obedience and chastity. The people of God were left to choose between "normal Christian living" (at a very subnormal standard) or "the way of spiritual perfection" in a monastic movement that was deeply dedicated, but removed from culture and society. The monks and nuns presented a model other Christians admired but did not often imitate.

The medieval church was sometimes able to enforce conformity to outward Christian norms. But it failed to create a Messianic people who could build the kingdom of God. Instead, it operated as a kind of chaplaincy to the rat race of ordinary human experience. While most of the laity desperately pursued *survival* or *success,* good monks, nuns and priests sought first the kingdom of God in the ascetic way of perfection. (Note that Jesus says there are two weeds which choke the word of the kingdom and prevent its fruition: "the cares of the world and the delight in riches"—Mt 13:22.) The church's societal control enabled it to stamp the insignia of Christianity throughout the culture, illuminating life with glimpses of spiritual significance. But in attempting to gain or hold that control, the church came to conform more and more to the world.

Several dimensions of human development—scientific, cultural, artistic and spiritual—were locked out of the medieval synthesis. As deeply Christian as the culture was, it was still a straitjacket that restrained the growth of human creativity. New currents of thought, urging that humanity develop its ruling powers more widely in this life, began to appear in the late Middle Ages. The Aristotelian movement swept in, shifting the culture from Platonic passivity toward technological control. The Southern Renaissance urged the culture to turn from Christian norms to pagan sources. Northern Christian humanists also turned away from dogma, but they went to the Bible, "to the sources," for a diagnosis of the medieval problem.

In the sixteenth century, Christian humanists all over Europe were set afire by Luther's discovery of justification by grace through faith. These Reformers altered the shape of Christian spirituality so that in many ways the creative energies of the Messianic kingdom were set free.[2] Yet Luther's ideal of "the priesthood of all believers" was very poorly realized—perhaps because his followers were more members of a Protestant people-movement than believers in the Messiah.

In large measure, the Reformers simply tuned up the medieval model of individualistic spirituality, without refocusing the church's consciousness on the kingdom of God.[3] The economic factors behind the rise of nationalism and the growth of the middle class had made it possible for the Reformation to happen and to survive. Now these secular forces were difficult to harness and redirect. For Protestant laity, it was fearfully easy to slip back into the familiar pattern of "business as usual," with the Protestant clergy replacing the monks as a new and improved chaplaincy to the rat race.

The thesis of Otto Weber and R. H. Tawney that there is an affinity between Puritan Calvinism and the spirit of capitalism does not really seem to be true of authentic Puritans, since it has to use rather run-down post-Puritans like Benjamin Franklin for evidence.[4] But why did Puritanism tend to run down over the generations and produce figures like Franklin? Could it be that the Puritan founders put forward an impressive spiritual goal for parishioners, but one that still retained an ascetic distance from ordinary life and did not provide an over-arching kingdom goal to bracket together earth and heaven?

Edmund Morgan comments that the Puritan founders sought to spread Christ's kingdom through mission to the Indians and through the creation of a showcase of Reformed Christianity which would be a model for the rest of the church. But in the second and third generations this goal changed to the founding of family dynasties like that of Abraham, in which piety leads inevitably to prosperity.[5] This somewhat introverted Old Testament model of the Christian life could be realized fairly easily if one thought of Native Americans as Canaanites and viewed North America as the promised land. The unexpected result of following this model, however, was New England's spiritual decline. Cotton Mather commented that piety had begotten prosperity, and the daughter had devoured the mother.[6] The characteristic sins of secular America emerge here: covetousness, leading to affluence and independence, followed by religious formalism, leading to outright unbelief.

From this point onward, much of the American laity began to regard the church primarily as a chaplaincy paid to remind us to "seek first the kingdom of God" (without defining this very clearly), while we spend our main energies pursuing success, or at least avoiding failure. The real goals of upwardly mobile Protestantism can be seen in Lisa Birnbach's humorous volume called *The Official Preppy Handbook*, which idealizes the semi-apostate New England family, still glumly going through the motions of "the Puritan ethic" in a sort of twilight zone between Christianity and secularism in order to facilitate its summers on Martha's Vineyard.[7]

This explains, among other things, why so many American universities founded to nurture Christianity have collapsed so readily into secularism. We might attribute this to Enlightenment thought-pollution. But why do alumni casually permit their schools to change from nurseries of piety into institutions which at best try to appear religiously neutral? Because religious neutrality is a familiar policy in business life, because Old Ivy is such a fruitful source of business contacts for the dynastic offspring, and because its diplomas help guarantee worldly success.

The American laity has easily succumbed to the Enlightenment economics of Adam Smith, which holds that society runs well if people simply do what comes naturally and build their dynasties, seeking first the kingdom of self. Marxism, another side of Enlightenment humanism, accurately perceives that corrupt dynasties form liaisons with bad religion, keeping the masses in poverty by emphasizing hope in the afterlife. But Marxists so far have delivered only worse poverty in societies that cripple both human freedom and the expression of the Messianic kingdom.

Eras of Renewal and Kingdom Advance

This does not mean that the American church, or Christianity in general, has totally failed to achieve kingdom goals. Although the *models* of the church and theology have been weak, the church's *experience* of the risen Messiah has often had a powerful impact in advancing God's kingdom. The conquest of the Roman Empire by the infant church and the monastic outreach in world mission were marked achievements, though they were afterward subject to setbacks and decay.

When the world overwhelmed the kingdom impulse and transformed the church, movements of renewal and reform fought back. Despite its incompleteness, the Reformation built a foundation for later Protestant renewal movements. As H. Richard Niebuhr points out, Calvin's work in Geneva and subsequent movements of evangelical awakening reached toward the Messianic kingdom even though they did not fully articulate this goal.[8]

More recent studies have shown that this movement is much broader than the Calvinist stream Niebuhr explores. It seems to travel along several different historical lines. As spiritual awakening develops, it puts increasing stress on lay activism. In the high tides of spiritual awakening, the achievements of the laity occupy centerstage and the clergy move to the sidelines like the coaches at an athletic contest.[9]

The Reformer Martin Bucer, John Calvin's mentor, who wrote *De Regno Christi* (On the Reign of Christ), was perhaps the first to articulate the agenda for subsequent Protestant awakenings. Bucer called for simultaneous movement toward what I call *inreach* (continued reformation and spiritual renewal in the visible church) and *outreach* (expansion of the church in world missions). On the basis of Romans 11, Bucer predicted that the flourishing of established Christian churches ("the fullness of the Gentiles") would eventually produce communities of such beauty and spiritual reality that the Jews, God's ancient covenant people, would be moved to envy and persuaded that Jesus was indeed the Messiah.[10]

All subsequent movements of spiritual awakening reached toward these two goals, in the hope of establishing a flourishing world Christian community involving Jews and Gentiles on an equal basis, which they called "the Church's Happy State." Whatever their millennial views, all expected the church to become a more purified agent of promoting the Messianic rule within ordinary history, until the promised return of Jesus.

The two "born again" movements of the seventeenth century, Calvinist Puritanism and Lutheran Pietism, were both part of the awakening stream. The work of the Pietists Spener and Francke was very different from the world-fleeing emotional introversion which we find in later corruptions of this movement. Francke's world-embracing projects for social and educational reform outstripped early forms of Enlightenment humanism, while retaining a solid base of orthodox Christianity.[11]

Timothy Smith, Donald Dayton and Howard Snyder have shown the great contribution of Wesleyan Christianity to kingdom-centered Christianity.[12] Actually, the most powerful demonstration of the Messianic kingdom we have yet seen may be the impact of the Wesleyan phase of the Great Awakening on the British Empire. Beginning with the Wesleys in the 1730s, the renewal continued in the Second Evangelical Awakening under the converted slavetrader, John Newton, who took Anglican orders and organized an "Evangelical United Front," involving elements of almost every denomination in England.[13] Not only was the church revitalized, but major societal changes took place.

A single Anglican parish in Clapham, near London, contributed business leaders and the parliamentarian William Wilberforce, who could reach the levers of power in the Empire. While modern laity may feel they are doing well to keep their own spiritual sanity and reach a few of their peers in personal evangelism, the Clapham laity set out to change the face of England. They attacked moral corruption until the dissolute Regency period yielded to the Victorian era. They lived out an evangelical theology of liberation, moving beyond the redemption of individual souls to bring about the abolition of the slave trade and the release of slaves within the Empire (at a cost of 20,000,000 pounds to the British Treasury), deliverance from wage slavery on the home front, and the conversion of the British Empire from an instrument of colonial exploitation into a rail system for the delivery of the gospel.[14] Their successors attacked the abuses of the Industrial Revolution until child labor was abolished and public school for commoners became a reality.

No clearly articulated theology of the kingdom of God motivated this great surge of spiritual and social transformation. But its cutting edge was a laity detached from the struggle for success or survival in the kingdom of self, and committed to establishing the reign of Christ through their vocations. The Clapham leaders lived at a spiritual level considerably beyond anything we even suggest for laity today. They spent three hours daily in prayer—morning, noon and evening. They were not just donating a percentage of their incomes to the clergy; they lived simply on a fraction of their incomes and ploughed the rest of their funds into missions, evangelism and the struggle against slavery, illiteracy and degradation. Some of them lost their health and their fortunes before the struggle ended. Lord Shaftesbury, who fought long and hard against the evils of industrial capitalism in

England, lived on the brink of poverty most of his life. These men and women were for the most part Tories—the equivalent of modern Republicans—but their very conservatism helped them to carry out reform once they saw it was necessary. Most historians agree that the whole movement from Wesley through Shaftesbury delayed the Enlightenment in England and avoided its political corollary, violent revolution.[15]

This expression of the Messianic kingdom was paralleled in the American phase of the Second Great Awakening. C. C. Cole has remarked that after an initial movement of widespread popular evangelism, the awakening involved and combined five waves of subsequent activity: (1) a wave of development in home and foreign missions; (2) a wave of popular Christian literature to nurture converts; (3) a wave of establishing new educational institutions, or reasserting Christian influence in older schools, to consolidate and extend the awakening; (4) a wave of cleaning up moral corruption; (5) a wave promoting peace and social justice, especially the great crusade for the abolition of slavery.[16]

Unfortunately, Southern evangelical clergy and theologians lost their nerve, avoided challenging the economic concerns of the laity, and developed a doctrine now labeled heresy by their descendants: "the spirituality of the church." This notion states that the church should deal only with spiritual issues, and let political and social issues alone. Because of this heresy and because the Evangelical United Front became theologically divided, Americans had to shed blood to abolish slavery in the Civil War. Still, Alexis de Tocqueville and Philip Schaff agree that nineteenth-century America was the most Christianized society in the world, despite the fact that the church relied on spiritual influence and not political establishment to transform the culture.[17]

What has led us from this level of kingdom transformation to the present level of secularization in America? There are many answers to this question. Drastic shifts in theology played a major role. A theological movement which had a great vision for mobilizing the laity, dispensationalism, replaced older evangelical theologies. Despite helpful features, it denied the present relevance of the kingdom of

God. A theology which did not call the laity to live out the Sermon on the Mount, and which thought the ruin of the church and the decay of Western society were a necessary prelude to the return of Jesus, seemed tailor-made for Christians who would rather concentrate on spiritual matters and leave society alone. Meanwhile the liberal Protestant theology of Albrecht Ritschl correctly saw the kingdom as the foundation of biblical theology, but built a kingdom vision which was only a thinly disguised version of Enlightenment humanism. The opposition between the unsatisfactory alternatives, called "fundamentalism" and "modernism," further divided and confused the church in the twentieth century.[18]

Living for God's Kingdom

Many other factors explain the loss of kingdom impact in modern Western Christianity. But the most crucial weakness was the polarization of kingdom concerns within the church: the loss of interest in spiritual dynamics among those concerned for the social impact of Christianity, and the restriction of spiritual renewal to private and individual spheres among those still concerned about spirituality. The result has been that instead of ordering careers, families, businesses and governments around God's purposes, we have, at best, tried to talk about Jesus to others while investing our main energy in pursuing the same things as the world: survival, security and wealth. The church is seen as an enclave of spirituality apart from the struggle for worldly success. It is a restricted sphere in which God is permitted to rule; outside, we run things. No wonder the kingdom is largely invisible to Jewish observers—it stops at the boundaries of Christian church buildings!

Humanity has consistently tried to confine religion to its buildings. But as we have seen, the Jewish tabernacle was not just a shelter for the altar and the sacrifices; it was a diagram of the kingdom of God. Exiled from Eden, where God's presence pervaded the world, his people could still meet with him in the courtyard of the tabernacle. Inside the sanctuary, past a table with bread and wine and a burning lampstand, they might glimpse the holy of holies—a curtained, perfectly cubical room symbolizing God's perfect rule in the heavens, which only the high priest could enter once a year. Inside was the ark of the testimony, a box overlaid with gold containing the stone tablets of the Law. Above the box's cover (called the mercy seat), the Shekinah, the radiant presence of God, was enthroned between the wings of two angelic beings, symbolic of the guardians set to keep humanity out of Eden.

It was this blueprint of the universe that the Israelites carried with them in the wilderness and sent before their troops in the conquest of Palestine. The careful artistry and precious materials that went into its construction are emblems of the exalted task of building the kingdom. But even as Moses was receiving this pattern on Mount Sinai, the people of God were urging the clergy, in the person of Aaron, to take the gold and the jewels they had brought out of Egypt, which were designed to be used in the sanctuary, and turn them into an idol instead. When the laity is building Babel instead of the kingdom of God, it always pressures the clergy to help in this task.

At David's initiative, Solomon turned this portable map of the kingdom into a fixed edifice. The struggle to keep it free from the distortions of idolatry continued. It was defiled and destroyed, rebuilt, and then destroyed again in A.D. 70. Even before this, however, God had made it clear that he did not dwell in buildings made with human hands.

Heaven is my throne
    and the earth is my footstool;
what is the house which you would build for me,
    and what is the place of my rest? . . .
But this is the man to whom I will look,
    he that is humble and contrite in spirit,
    and trembles at my word. (Is 66:1-2)

God's home is the human heart that is sensitive to his voice. The ark of the covenant is a symbol for lives which will be transformed under the New Covenant: "I will sprinkle clean water upon you, and you shall be clean from all your uncleanness, and from all your idols I will cleanse you. A new heart I will give you, and a new spirit I will put within you; and I will take out of your flesh the heart of stone and give you a heart of flesh. And I will put my spirit within you, and cause you to walk in my statutes and be careful to observe my ordinances" (Ezek 36:25-27). The will of God, the central determinant of the presence of the kingdom, is now "written . . . with the Spirit of the living God, not on tablets of stone but on tablets of human hearts" (2 Cor 3:3).

Thus, Jesus, unlike Solomon, has permanently fulfilled God's promise to David: he has not only made our bodies into temples in which God dwells (1 Cor 6:19), but he has built these together "like living stones . . . into a spiritual house" (1 Pet 2:5 NIV), which is his mystical body. At the close of history we will return to the condition of Eden, immersed in the presence of God, with no need to meet him in a specific temple or church. But our dwelling then will not be a garden. The perfect cube of the inmost sanctuary of the temple is now presented as a city built to the same proportions, the New Jerusalem, the City of the Peace of Yahweh. "And I saw no temple in the city, for its temple is the Lord God the Almighty and the Lamb. And the city has no need of sun or moon to shine upon it, for the glory of God is its light, and its lamp is the Lamb" (Rev 21:22-23; see also Is 60:19).

The creation of this perfectly God-centered world is far beyond our power and skill. It requires the direct intervention of God in history, reconstructing our mortal bodies and releasing our planet from bondage and distortion (1 Cor 15:50). This release and reconstruction can only occur with the visible return of Christ, and the creation of "new heavens and a new earth in which righteousness dwells."

Even so, our every goal and action should anticipate this God-centered world. Everything we are and do should point to this coming realm and model it before the rest of the world. Christians should build straight houses in the midst of a world where crooked people are building crooked homes. They should run straight businesses, and vote for straight government, in a world where these structures are misshapen by human sin. Their lives should appear to the world as centers of divine righteousness, peace and joy.

Obviously kingdom-centered living does not come easily. In a world which constantly conditions us to seek personal success as producer-consumers, we easily lose sight of our goal. Our whole educational system, with its competitive patterns, is aimed not so much to reward

us with personal fulfillment as to make us maximally efficient, inter-
changeable parts for the machinery of production. Even the church
is infected with status seeking and empire building at the expense of
concern for the kingdom of God. It is not easy for us to come to
ourselves, as David did, and wake up to the fact that we are organizing
our lives around personal goals rather than around God's kingdom:
"See now, I dwell in a house of cedar, but the ark of God dwells in
a tent" (2 Sam 7:2). Only rarely do we wake up like Solomon to
acknowledge that our first request from God should not be for wealth,
riches or honor, but for wisdom to govern adequately that small part
of his maturing kingdom which is our province (2 Chron 1:8-12).

In the secularized public educational system, we are literally conditioned to become builders of Babel instead of shapers of the kingdom of God. Everything around us tells us to work on an *individual*
"tower with its top in the heavens, and . . . make a name for ourselves"
through professional success (Gen 11:4). The divided condition of
American life, as we work frantically to build millions of dynastic
towers, may be preferable to merging all these competing power centers in one great secular Babel, as Communists have tried to do. But
it creates a force field of individualism which affects the church,
where empire building shatters catholic unity and creates waste and
chaos. With the coming of the Holy Spirit at Pentecost, humanity can
be unified in the Messianic kingdom without the danger of building
Babel. But it often seems that the church is as divided as any other
institution in our society. Its leaders often conform to the world, concentrating on success and reputation at the expense of the health of
the whole body of Christ.

But God has a way of frustrating our personal goals until they are
reorganized with his kingdom at the center. This process is described
in the prophecy of Haggai:

> Thus says the LORD of hosts: This people say the time has not yet
> come to rebuild the house of the LORD. . . . Is it a time for you
> yourselves to dwell in your paneled houses, while this house lies
> in ruins? . . . Consider how you have fared. You have sown much,
> and harvested little; you eat, but you never have enough; you drink,
> but you never have your fill; you clothe yourselves, but no one is

warm; and he who earns wages earns wages to put them into a bag with holes. . . . Consider how you have fared. Go up to the hills and bring wood and build the house, that I may take pleasure in it and that I may appear in my glory, says the LORD. You have looked for much, and, lo, it came to little; and when you brought it home, I blew it away. Why? says the LORD of hosts. Because of my house that lies in ruins, while you busy yourselves each with his own house. Therefore the heavens above you have withheld the dew, and the earth has withheld its produce. And I have called for a drought upon the land. (1:2-11)

This is an apt description of the economic difficulties the world is experiencing today. These conditions are not just a challenge to non-Christians. They are also a judgment on styles of Christianity that do not seek first the kingdom of God, but operate instead as chaplaincies to those involved in the rat race for success. Much of our current search for inner fulfillment is only a spiritual form of this same self-centeredness. What would happen if the energy directed toward these disguised forms of self-betterment were turned instead to the betterment of the kingdom? Then perhaps we should see the fulfillment of God's encouraging words through Haggai to a people who were turning to build the house of God:

Who is left among you that saw this house in its former glory? How do you see it now? Is it not in your sight as nothing? Yet now take courage . . . all you people of the land, says the LORD; work, for I am with you, says the LORD of hosts, according to the promise that I made you. . . . My Spirit abides among you; fear not. For thus says the LORD of hosts: Once again, in a little while, I will shake the heavens and the earth and the sea and the dry land; and I will shake all nations, so that the treasures of all nations shall come in, and I will fill this house with splendor, says the LORD of hosts. . . . The latter splendor of this house shall be greater than the former, says the LORD of hosts; and in this place I will give prosperity, says the LORD of hosts. (2:3-9)

Discussion Questions

Recommended supplemental reading: chapter 1 in *Dynamics*. Scripture for meditation: Matthew 6:16-34; 13:31-52.

1. What difficulties do we face today in fulfilling Christ's command to love our neighbor as ourselves?

2. In your experience, how much emphasis is given to the kingdom of God in today's Christianity?

3. How important a theme in Scripture is the kingdom of God?

4. Why do most Christians fail to relate their daily experience to Christ's kingdom?

5. How is it possible to make our lives more kingdom-centered?

6. What would a kingdom-centered church be like?

7. If the church became more kingdom-centered, what differences might this make in our impact on the world?

Part II
Dynamics of
Spiritual Death

The Flesh

3

All who attempt for a single day to lead a life centered on God and his kingdom will discover that they have a battle on their hands. This ideal is simply not a possibility for human nature. We do not have in ourselves the wellsprings of a love which will delight in God and constantly seek to obey his will. Nor are we able to care for others as we care for ourselves. Often when we try to do so, the inner struggle becomes so intense that we end up uglier people than before we started.

The reason these goals are not easily attained is that we live in a fallen world, a world which has moved away from the reign of God and come under the dominion of other powers. Everything in this world, and especially our fallen human nature, resists the rulership of God. Unless God changes our hearts, we are actively allergic to him! We are like the child whose body rejects milk, but needs it to survive. The roots of this allergic resistance are what Donald Mostrom has called "the negative factors in Christian experience," which are classically summarized as "the world, the flesh and the devil."[1]

It is vital that we understand these forces, for they are the main obstacles to spiritual renewal. Later we will discuss the dynamics of spiritual life, but these factors are *dynamics of spiritual death.* Together they form what Walter Rauschenbusch called "the Kingdom of Evil," which resists and wars against the kingdom of God.[2] That resistance is localized in the individual heart, in what we call *the flesh,* although it is influenced and directed by forces outside the individual: *the world* and *the devil.*

Paul connects all of these together in a text contrasting the natural state of spiritual death with the condition of new life entered through faith in the Messiah: "And you he made alive, when you were dead through the trespasses and sins in which you once walked, following the course of this world, following the prince of the power of the air, the spirit that is now at work in the children of disobedience" (Eph 2:1-2). In the next three chapters we will discuss these factors, following the order used in this verse—the flesh, the world and the devil—since it most clearly indicates the real power structure of the kingdom of evil.

The Depth of Human Sin

Paul goes on in Ephesians to comment, "We all once lived in the passions of our flesh, following the desires of body and mind, and so we were by nature children of wrath, like the rest of mankind" (2:3). The rather lurid phrase "passions of our flesh" catches our eye in this passage, suggesting sexual sin (America's favorite and almost only recognized form of depravity). But this phrase is not properly identified with any one sin or with any sinful actions as such. It is rather the Bible's word for the drive behind all sins. The *flesh* is simply one of several words Scripture uses to describe fallen human nature.

Few people in the world today, and even fewer in the church, think of themselves as sinners—those driven by the "passions of the flesh." But Ephesians 2 is uncompromisingly negative: apart from Christ, we are "children of disobedience," born with a constant urge to disobey.

Ephesians warns that it may not be difficult for us to go on behaving that way, even after we have come to Christ (Eph 4:17-19).

Today's non-Christians, encouraged by popular psychologies which accentuate positive thinking and self-acceptance, think of themselves as fundamentally good people trying to do the right thing but missing the mark occasionally. Even if they are uncommitted to God, they see themselves as honest searchers for evidence of his existence, not as rebels continually crossing the street to avoid meeting him.

Many Christians also are inclined to think that sin is a rare exception in their lives. They define it as occasional acts of willful disobedience to known laws of God, such as the Ten Commandments. In this definition sin is reduced to conscious rebellious actions—major transgressions with serious consequences.

Now it is obvious that this view screens out most of the serious sin in our lives. In concentrating on *actions,* we uncover only the tip of the iceberg. Overlooked are our sinful *attitudes,* the continuing resistance to God's will which give rise to actions. Biblical definitions of sin give much more prominence to attitudes or continuous patterns of behavior than to isolated acts.

Paul's list of "the works of the flesh" in Galatians 5:19-21, for instance, includes some items which are actions: sexual immorality, debauchery, fits of rage, drunkenness and orgies. But it includes more items which are attitudes or complex patterns of behavior which are mixtures of inner drives and acts: impurity, idolatry, witchcraft, hatred, discord, jealousy, selfish ambition, dissensions, factions and envy. In Ephesians 4:26-31 Paul warns against harboring continued anger toward others, thus giving the devil a kind of gun emplacement from which to fire at them. In Colossians 3:5 and 1 Corinthians 6:5 he warns against covetousness, an itch for possessions, a sin which pervades our lives because it is almost institutionalized in the American economy.

Jesus evidently believed it essential for the establishment of his kingdom to shake people out of the easy self-righteousness that conceives of virtue only as avoiding vicious acts. The Sermon on the Mount is a dose of cold water thrown to wake us out of this delusion, condemning lust and hatred as tantamount to adultery and murder.

Our conventional moralism with its check lists of duties to be done and acts to be avoided is an easy game to win. But it is only a shallow form of pharisaism—and Jesus warned, "unless your righteousness surpasses that of the Pharisees . . . you will certainly not enter the kingdom of heaven" (Mt 5:20 NIV). We get the full impact of this challenge when we consider that the word *Pharisee* literally means "Puritan," and that it connotes serious ethical earnestness and strong orthodoxy. The Pharisees were not empty hypocrites, but the most dedicated religious persons of their time.

Another way to gauge the depth of sin in our experience is to reflect on the Bible's standard of optimal spirituality, its picture of the holy life. We have already seen this set forth in the Old Testament in Deuteronomy 6:4 and restated in the New Testament by Jesus: "You shall love the Lord your God with all your heart, and with all your soul, and with all your mind, and with all your strength. . . . You shall love your neighbor as yourself" (Mk 12:30-31 NASB). This is a large order! The second part is not quite so easy to forget, since we are constantly bumping up against neighbors. But how often during the day are we actually conscious of thinking about God, let alone loving him with heart, soul, mind and strength?

Awareness of God and his biblical directives for our lives ought to be the constant horizon in our consciousness, a background for everything that we are doing in the foreground. When events shake us and issues demand choices, we should always respond as agents of the Messianic kingdom—"having the mind of Christ," informed and empowered by his Spirit and instructed by relevant passages from his Word, called out of memory by the Spirit. And our responses should not be halting and half-hearted, but rapid and vigorous, proceeding from a pure heart and not from mixed motives.

The clergy do not often commend this level of commitment and experience to laypeople. Usually they make excuses for the hours of spiritual amnesia we spend each day ignoring God and his will. But according to Paul, "everything that does not come from faith is sin" (Rom 14:23 NIV). This does not necessarily mean that we must consciously make our every thought and act reflect our Christian beliefs. It does mean that in a life which is truly filled with the Holy Spirit and the Word of God, acts and thoughts and emotions will constantly be created and controlled by the Spirit. From time to time, we will be aware that they are centered on God and his kingdom.

Looking at the depth of sin on the one hand, and the height of holiness on the other, our first impulse may be to throw up our hands and quote Paul: "Who is sufficient for these things?" (2 Cor 2:16). It has been argued that too much reflection on the depth of our sin will produce a spiritually paralyzing guilt trip. Some powerful voices have urged us to ignore the negative factors in Christian experience and to concentrate on positive thinking about our spiritual and material possibilities. And Christian psychologists have warned us that without a positive self-image, we will have little ability to love God and others.

There is certainly truth in these affirmations. Human nature as God made it is full of the potential for grandeur. It is a ruined palace, as Augustine says, but it is still a palace, as great as Versailles or Fontaine-bleau. Fallen human beings at their worst are full of gifts and a certain dark nobility. This is why God gave his Son to redeem them, and why he pursues them relentlessly, as the love of Donna Elvira pursued Don Giovanni to the very brink of hell. Look at the gifts displayed by godless people and the success that God often showers on them. He is not simply mocking them and designing an ironic ending to their story. For he is not willing that any should perish, but that all should come to repentance (2 Pet 3:9). He is pursuing them to the end, pleading his love with blessings, and proving it also by sorrows and setbacks that are meant to awaken them. If God is wrestling with every human being on earth to bring him or her to salvation, allowing each to exercise some gifts and gain some victories, we must be creatures of great value even in our fallen state. Only the devil can rail at sinners. We must treat them with respect.

And that is true also as we look at ourselves. If our sins weigh heavier in our mind than our potential for grace and effective service to God and others, we must be taking the devil's perspective. God wants us to be realistic about ourselves. But genuine realism does not lead to caving in under a sense of worthlessness. That is not realism; it is believing the devil's lie. Yes, realism leads us to a sense of weakness. But it leads also to Paul's assertion: "I can do all things through

Christ who strengthens me" (Phil 4:13). Paul says elsewhere, "He said to me, 'My grace is sufficient for you, for my power is made perfect in weakness.' I will all the more gladly boast of my weaknesses, that the power of Christ may rest upon me. For the sake of Christ, then, I am content with weaknesses . . . for when I am weak, then I am strong" (2 Cor 12:9-10).

Christians whose spiritual lives are grounded and nurtured *only* on self-esteem and positive thinking, without a vision of the depth of sin, are going to be lacking in depth, reality and humility. Spirituality is imparted by the Holy Spirit, and since he is "the Spirit of truth" (Jn 14:17), he cannot dwell in fullness where there is only partial openness to truth. If we cannot face the bad news about the depth of sin and the height of holiness, we cannot fully grasp the good news of salvation and the transformed life in Christ.

The vision of the depth of our sin, as in the case of Isaiah's vision in the temple, purges us, by convincing us of our sinfulness, and by cleansing us from it. It breaks our callousness and our spiritual pride. Christians who are sensitive to the depth of their sin are a lot easier to be with, because they are not as inclined to be judgmental. As Jonathan Edwards observes:

> Spiritual pride is very apt to suspect others; whereas an humble saint is most jealous of himself, he is so suspicious of nothing in the world as he is of his own heart. The spiritually proud person is apt to find fault with other saints, that they are low in grace; and to be much in observing how cold and sad they are; and being quick to discern and take notice of their deficiencies. But the eminently humble Christian has so much to do at home, and sees so much evil in his own heart, and is so concerned about it, that he is not apt to be very busy with other hearts. . . . He is apt to esteem others better than himself, and is ready to hope that there is nobody but what has more love and thankfulness to God than he, and cannot bear to think that others should bring forth no more fruit to God's honour than he. . . . Pure Christian humility disposes a person to take notice of every thing that is good in others, and to make the best of it, and to diminish their failings; but to have his eye chiefly on those things that are bad in himself, and to take

much notice of every thing that aggravates them.[3]
There may be a bit of Augustinian overkill in this statement—a
danger of the ascetic confusion of low self-esteem with the mortifica-
tion of pride and the pursuit of humility—but there is also a real
description of saintly humility.

Many times I have observed spiritual growth in others begin with
such a sobering vision of the depth of personal sin. Such "dark nights
of the soul" can be painful and even terrifying, but they are also
purifying—"purgatory arriving early," as Luther said.[4] It takes time to
get used to living with the clear truth about ourselves. But nothing else
is so effective in teaching us to rely on the righteousness of Jesus the
Messiah to commend us to God.

Edwards saw a whole town gripped by Isaiah's vision during the
Great Awakening—a simultaneous awareness of the glory of God and
the identity and seriousness of its sins—and he saw the town purged
as a result. In every subsequent awakening, deep conviction of sin has
worked upon large numbers of people, resulting in broad changes in
society. When great numbers of Christians straighten out crooked
patterns of living, and start making a prophetic and evangelistic ap-
peal to those around them, a culture can be shaken to its foundations.
Perhaps the shallow results of the current evangelical and charismatic
resurgence spring from a spirituality which takes a detour around the
vision of sin in order to grasp at psychological and material comfort.

Yes, we need a positive image of the renewed life we have in Christ.
But Paul's vision of himself was uncompromisingly realistic: "Christ
Jesus came into the world to save sinners—of whom I am the worst"
(1 Tim 1:15 NIV); "For I know that nothing good dwells within me,
that is, in my flesh" (Rom 7:18).

Understanding the Flesh

This brings us back again to Paul's term "the flesh." At first glance
it seems a confusing term. Does Paul mean that the body is the source
of evil, as the Greeks and the Gnostics believed? Does he believe that
"carnal" sins—like sexual immorality—are the worst? The answer in
both cases is no.

Even in Scripture, "the flesh" has several meanings. Sometimes it

simply refers to humanity without any overtones of sinfulness (Gen
2:24; Ps 145:21). Occasionally, particularly in the Old Testament, it
symbolizes the weakness of human nature ("All flesh is grass. . . . The
grass withers, the flower fades"—Is 40:6-7 NASB).

In the New Testament, however, are many places where the term
has a darker coloring. Here it refers primarily to the whole human
personality—body, soul, mind and emotions as they function apart
from the presence and control of the Holy Spirit. It can refer either
to non-Christians or to residual sin in believers. Although Paul clearly
teaches that through our union with Christ in his death and resurrection, the central control of sin has been broken in our lives (Rom 6:2-
6), he also teaches that until our bodies are transformed we continue
to struggle with remainders of sin: "So I find it to be a law that when
I want to do right, evil lies close at hand. For I delight in the law of
God, in my inmost self, but I see in my members another law at war
with the law of my mind and making me captive to the law of sin
which dwells in my members. Wretched man that I am! Who will
deliver me from this body of death? Thanks be to God through Jesus
Christ our Lord!" (Rom 7:21-25).

Some Christians believe that this applies only to non-Christians,
and that believers do not experience such struggles. But this is an
unrealistic view both of Christians—we do have such battles—and of
non-Christians, not many of whom "delight in the law of God." Elsewhere, Paul clearly teaches that this tug of war goes on in believers.
"Walk by the Spirit, and do not gratify the desires of the flesh. For the
desires of the flesh are against the Spirit, and the desires of the Spirit
are against the flesh; for these are opposed to each other, to prevent
you from doing what you would. But if you are led by the Spirit you
are not under the law" (Gal 5:16-18).

Paul is contrasting here a way of life which is still "under the law,"
which relies on will power rather than on the Messiah. This is why
he thanks God through Christ for deliverance in Romans 7 and urges
us to walk by the Spirit of Christ in Galatians 5. The contrast in
Romans 7 is not between a non-Christian way of life and a Christian
one, but between a Christian life which is ignoring the dynamics of
life in Christ, and one which is aware of these and drawing on them

through faith in the Messiah.

The origin of the flesh is described in the account of the Fall (Gen 3). The devil appeals to certain God-given drives in the woman: the drive for rulership ("You will be like God, knowing good and evil"— Gen 3:5); and the drive for sensory gratification ("The woman saw that the tree was good for food, and that it was a delight to the eyes"— Gen 3:6). But he argues that these should be exercised in a way that is independent of God the Creator, a way which deprives God of his legitimate role as supreme Lord and lawgiver. In fact, he really invites the woman to block out of her consciousness the true picture of God as infinitely wise and good and holy. He invites her to give up the truth that God is an infinitely kind and powerful friend, and exchange this for the lie that God is a grudging enemy whose power is limited and whose judgment can be evaded.

The central action of the Fall, and the core of the flesh, is a movement from light into darkness, from a world of truth to a universe based on lies. The characteristic movement of the flesh is to pursue real goods (power, wisdom, sensual gratification) according to legitimate, God-implanted drives, but to do so apart from God, refusing to restrain and direct our drives according to his will.

At the center of the flesh is the reflex action of repressing God, shunning the knowledge of the one whose rule should control all our actions. Of course, we may substitute an idol, a fictitious god who will support our goals or allow us room to indulge our desires. As Paul says, "The wrath of God is revealed from heaven against all ungodliness and wickedness of men who by their wickedness suppress the truth. For what can be known about God is plain to them" through the visible grandeur of the creation. But "although they knew God they did not honor him as God or give thanks to him, but they became futile in their thinking and their senseless minds were darkened. Claiming to be wise, they became fools, and exchanged the glory of the immortal God for images resembling mortal man or birds or animals or reptiles" (Rom 1:18-19, 21-23).

In the late nineteenth century, many Christians believed that it was possible for believers to live a perfect life without sin. They were able to believe this because they had redefined sin as conscious willful acts of disobedience to known laws. Just at the time when Christians were becoming shallow in their understanding of human behavior, modern psychology began to develop much deeper insights. Sigmund Freud recovered the biblical understanding that people's conscious reasons for their acts were less important than their unconscious motivations, and that many of these were dark and amoral. Freud also uncovered the truth that human beings repress traumatic events and facts, pushing these down into the unconscious—although Freud failed to realize that he himself was repressing the most supremely traumatic fact of all: his rebellion against the true God.

Subsequent schools of psychology have shown us more and more about the drives that move human beings, both Christians and non-Christians. Freud had stressed the importance of the sex drive and the other life-supporting appetites. Adler emphasized the drive to power, superiority, dominion. Jung indicated that we have also an inborn desire to achieve the integration of personality through religious experience—a hunger for the divine, as Augustine believed, despite our fallen nature's allergy to God. Erich Fromm uncovered a drive for freedom, while also stressing our needs for affirming personal relationships, rational creativity, rootedness or belonging, a sense of personal identity, and a rational framework of understanding ourselves and the world. Among the Third Force, or humanistic psychologists, Abraham Maslow posited a "hierarchy of needs" ranging from the primitive drives of thirst and hunger through drives toward safety, security, love, belongingness, self-esteem, knowledge and beauty.

All of these theorists have something to teach us about what moves human nature, about the make-up of "the desires of the flesh." We need to recognize that these drives in themselves are good and implanted by God. The ascetic Christian tradition tended to mistake these drives for sin itself and sought to lower self-esteem, for instance, in order to conquer pride. But what is wrong with the flesh is not these legitimate desires, which must be satisfied in any healthy personality. The problem is the *disordering* of these drives by the sin principle, which insists that they be exercised apart from any awareness of God and any restraining control of the Holy Spirit.

Viewed in this light, every major vice is only an unnatural exaggeration of a legitimate virtue. The drive toward power or self-esteem, if unchecked, becomes the sin of pride. The drive for healthy sexual gratification becomes promiscuity or perverted lust. The religious drive becomes the worship of creatures or false images of God. Sometimes these disordered drives interact with one another, cross-pollinate, and we get the man who uses a woman both to satisfy lust and to gain prestige, power or money (which conveys the power to satisfy all drives to excess). Every fallen personality is therefore a caricature of what it should be, with some parts dwarfed and others enlarged and distorted.

"The desires of the flesh," however, have something more behind them as an innocent animal nature devoid of the Holy Spirit. Animals follow their instincts without consulting God, and without sin or guilt. But our indulgence of these drives has a deeper, underlying motivation: the compulsion not to believe God and to rebel against him. Every vice is therefore more than simple weakness. It has the bitter undertaste of rebellion and the poison of unbelief, which Luther believed was the deepest root of all sin.

It is not hard, therefore, to "walk in the flesh." All we have to do is "do what comes naturally" in the most literal sense—do whatever we feel like doing, without asking how God feels about our behavior. When we "walk in the Spirit," on the other hand, we are constantly, almost unconsciously, measuring our thoughts and feelings and acts against biblical principles illuminated by the Holy Spirit, and drawing on his power to order and direct these according to the will of God.

"Walking in the flesh," then, does not necessarily produce violence or rampant immorality. Thoroughly respectable non-Christians can be walking in the flesh all the time simply because their lives are determined by a delicate balance of natural drives, uninfluenced by any desire to please God. Their basic motivation may simply be to hang onto respectability, a need based on the desire for self-esteem and the affection of others. In fact, their "goodness" may be just another one of their weapons against God, designed to prove that they do not need to serve or even believe in him in order to be good. There will be a certain deadness about their goodness. But their lives may be more righteous in outward actions, though not in motivation, than those of most Christians.

It is unsettling for Christians to recognize that parts of their own behavior may be made up of this "dead goodness." In reality, all the righteousness we achieve in ordinary history is a mixture of divine and human motives, which is why Scripture says that "all our right-eousnesses are as filthy rags" (Is 64:6 KJV).

In the television film *Holocaust,* a leader in the Hitler regime is shown enjoying all the familiar joys of Christmas with his family, when we know all along that he is involved in a system devoted to war and genocide. Some viewers were angry because the Nazis were por-trayed as "too nice," too ordinary and respectable—too much like us! The banality of evil is something we forget. We can be moral and respectable, while at the same time we are involved in businesses or societies which are oppressing others by pursuing corporate self-in-terest. This adds a whole new dimension to our perception of sin and guilt. There is a corporate guilt we bear because of our participation in crooked systems, though our own lives may be straight by ordinary standards. Unless the Holy Spirit breaks through our conventional behavior with the conviction that we are involved in things that are opposed to God's kingdom, we will inevitably continue sleepwalking in sin.

How can we bear up under the full and realistic vision of our individual and corporate sins? The remedy is Luther's discovery of justification by grace through faith in Jesus the Messiah. Luther, like all the Reformers, insisted on being realistic about the sin in his life. But a medieval theology of individual merit combined with a realistic view of sin could only lead him to despair. Finally he made a break-through: he discovered that "the righteousness of God revealed from faith to faith" (Rom 1:17 KJV) was wholly based upon the righteous-ness of Christ. He found that the end of this verse, "the just shall live by faith," meant that we become righteous as we believe in Jesus the Messiah. Jesus' perfect righteousness is then imputed or imposed on our very imperfect record. The result is suggested by part of a poem by Gerard Manley Hopkins:

Across my foundering deck shone

A beacon, an eternal beam. Flesh fade, and mortal trash

Fall to the residuary worm; world's wildfire, leave but ash:
   In a flash, at a trumpet crash,
I am all at once what Christ is, since he was what I am, and
This Jack, joke, poor potsherd, patch, matchwood,
   immortal diamond
   Is immortal diamond.[5]

Hopkins was writing about our transformation at the time of resurrection. But these words can also convey Luther's understanding of the way we become righteous before God. Because we are "accepted in the beloved" (Eph 1:6 KJV), everything that was his is now accounted ours, including his perfect obedience to God and his expiation of our sin upon the cross.

Thus the way back into fellowship with God retravels the road humanity took when we fell away from him. We went away from the light of truth into the darkness of a world of lies. We return by turning from darkness and facing the bitter truth about our sin—and the glorious truth about his love toward us in Christ. A clear vision of sin will not debilitate us if it is matched by a clear view of our acceptance through the perfect righteousness of Jesus the Messiah. As John says: "God is light and in him is no darkness at all. If we say we have fellowship with him while we walk in darkness, we lie and do not live according to the truth; but if we walk in the light, as he is in the light, we have fellowship with one another, and the blood of Jesus his Son cleanses us from all sin. If we say we have no sin, we deceive ourselves, and the truth is not in us. If we confess our sins, he is faithful and just, and will forgive our sins and cleanse us from all unrighteousness" (1 Jn 1:5-9).

We can face the bad news about our sin if we also keep before us the good news of our acceptance in Christ. We need to keep our gaze fixed on the positive realities of grace, on what we have going for us in Christ (the subject of later sections of this book).

Walking with God is essentially a positive thing. The Bible does not point us toward constant introspection. Instead, it helps us to focus on the privileges of being in Christ and enjoying fellowship with God. This is the emphasis we have already seen in Paul: "Walk in the Spirit, and you will not fulfill the desires of the flesh." If we concentrate on fellowship with the Spirit and are led by him, then we will not be overcome and carried out of God's will by natural drives. While this perspective is important and refreshing, it remains true that there *is* conflict in us between the Spirit and the flesh. If we are wholly unaware of our characteristic patterns of fleshly behavior, these are likely to remain master of our lives. It is important that we be able to discern the shape of our weaknesses and recognize our flesh when it is struggling to assert itself.

Discerning Our Flesh

Detecting our characteristic sins—what Puritans called our "besetting sins"—can be difficult. These patterns of motivation and behavior are elusive. We have settled down and gotten used to them; our consciences are dulled to their existence the same way our ears adjust to background noises, or our noses to bad odors. Others are aware of them, but often do not share this insight. Or they may tell us in ways that threaten or intimidate us, which only makes the problem worse. Beyond this, however, we are *afraid* to see the whole scope of our need. It would produce too much guilt or bury us under a mountain of insoluble problems.

But the priestly work of the Messiah has freed us from these problems so that we can experience his kingly rule in and through our lives. A clearly stated ideal in the New Testament is that all believers should live as free persons. Galatians 5, the Christian's Magna Carta, reminds us that this is one of the greatest aims of Jesus' work in our behalf: "It is for freedom that the Messiah has set us free. Stand firm, then, and do not let yourselves be burdened again by a yoke of slavery. . . . You, my brothers, were called to be free" (Gal 5:1, 13 NIV). Looking forward to that freedom, we should have no fear in examining closely the bonds his power must break to set us free.

One of these characteristics is confirmed hostility toward God and his truth. "The mind set on the flesh is hostile toward God; for it does not subject itself to the law of God, for it is not even able to do so" (Rom 8:7 NASB). *Unbelief* is the deepest root of sin, and we become aware of our rebellious lack of faith when we fall short of some clear promise or command of God. Thus there must be regular contact with the Word of God, including private reading and meditation, or there can be little discernment of the operation of the flesh. We are always prone to slide away from a sharp awareness of our flesh. But Scripture is like a mirror which shocks us back into being conscious of how we really appear to God (Jas 1:22-25). Hostility to biblical truth, or an aversion to reading or hearing any part of Scripture, is invariably a mark of the flesh.

The flesh is deeply *self-centered.* Ultimately it looks at all issues from a selfish perspective. "What's in it for me?" is the question it invariably asks. It produces many ingenious compounds: self-confidence, self-consciousness, self-importance, self-indulgence, self-pity, self-righteousness, self-satisfaction, self-fulfillment. There is a legitimate and God-inspired sense of pride in self-worth. But what we see in magazines, like the one named *Self,* is something else: it is either rebellion declaring itself, or despair whistling in the dark.

As we have indicated, the flesh is deeper than the surface actions of sin. It is really a *complex* of deep, compelling drives beneath our acts and thoughts and emotions. "Walking in the Spirit" is like being a musical instrument in the hands of a master musician, playing Beethoven according to the composer's instructions. "Walking in the flesh" is like struggling with a player piano which insists on playing something other than the score. At other times, it is simply being unconscious of sin while we are swept along on a torrent of self-absorbed desire, fear, envy, anxiety or hostility. Most serious operations of the flesh are not pleasant acts of sin. They are states and attitudes which are painful even to *us!*—sins like worry, resentment, envy and jealousy. "Walking in the flesh" is not necessarily a result of conscious sinful choices. Often we walk in the flesh simply by neglecting to "walk in the Spirit."

The flesh can develop a high degree of refinement or religiosity. Spiritual pride, heroic self-abasement, partisan zeal, dogmatic rigor and sentimental doctrinal indifference are all works of the flesh. We are seldom eager to have our real patterns of sin exposed and put to death. So we construct pleasant substitutes, or sublimate our self-centeredness into "spiritual" forms. Carnal religiosity is at best ugly— when it produces persons who are so self-consciously "spiritual" that they set our teeth on edge—and at worst highly destructive—when it inspires religious persecution, division and party spirit, or empire building in the church.

The flesh is often attached to idols of some sort. The idol may be ourselves, other persons (a parent, spouse or child), humanity or the state (as in atheistic communism). Or we may idolize some possession or activity. Our economic system is geared to stir up "covetousness, which is idolatry" (Col 3:5). Business and advertising work together to promote this and other expressions of the flesh. The most blatant form of *religious flesh* is nonbiblical religion, in which a false god is worshiped, or the true God is maligned by cultic life or heretical doctrine. Carnal religiosity can also take the form of "spilt religion," in which devotion that ought to be given to God and his kingdom alone is diverted and fixed on religious leaders (whether dead or alive), particular denominations, doctrinal traditions constructed by individuals, local congregations or religious projects. When the unity, purity or peace of the church is shattered, there is usually idolatry involved somewhere.

Only by turning to God and following his direction through the guidance of his Spirit and his Word can we hope to deal with our flesh. And only by fully understanding the depth of our sin can we begin to deal with the other negative influences on our life: the world and the devil.

Discussion Questions

Recommended supplemental reading: chapter 3 in *Dynamics*. Scripture for meditation: Galatians 5:16-26.

1. How do most Christians today define and understand sin?

2. In your opinion, what added dimensions of sin is it important for us to understand? Why?

3. What does Paul mean by "the flesh"?

4. What does it mean to "walk in the flesh" or "walk in the Spirit"?

5. Are there any dangers in introspection, in thinking too much about our sin? How can we avoid these and still be realistic?

6. How important is it for us to maintain a positive self-image? How can we do this and still be realistic about our sin?

7. What is *corporate sin?* What corporate sins are you aware of today?

The World

4

The second traditional obstacle to spiritual renewal is the world. Today, this negative factor in Christian experience is poorly understood and usually goes unmentioned. Occasionally the term surfaces in very conservative Protestant circles, where it is treated in a way that does not do justice to Scripture nor to our understanding of psychology, sociology and economics.

Modern theologians in the last few decades have ignored the world as a source of problems. Instead, they seem to have embraced it as a model or guide and as a fountainhead of important questions which Christians should be answering. In the 1960s, some Christians seemed to compete with one another in the game of being "worldlier than thou."

And in thrusts toward human liberation, such as the civil rights movement, it is partly true that the world outside the church often sets the agenda and forges ahead toward justice in ways which put the church to shame. Paradoxically, I believe this has been due to the worldliness of the church!—in the biblical sense of the word. For unless the church can escape conformity to the world, it will inevitably make it necessary for God to perform many vital services for humanity through "secular humanists" instead of through his chosen people. "The kingdom of the world" will not become "the kingdom of our Lord and of his Messiah" (Rev 11:15) until the church shakes off this conformity and assumes her proper role in history.

What the World Is Not

Since the end of the last century, *worldliness* for many Christians has meant certain activities that characterize the world outside the church but that are not supposed to be allowed within it: drinking alcoholic beverages, smoking, dancing, attending movies, playing cards, wearing cosmetics and other activities which are not "kosher" for Christians. Anyone behaving in these ways is assumed to be "going native" and backsliding spiritually.

Some of these activities were condemned by the early church fathers as occasions of sin for Christians (dancing, cosmetics, the theater). The English Puritans took these scruples, which had been held only by very zealous Catholics, and made them the rule for everyone in the church—adding card playing, on the grounds that it depended on "chance" and thus violated the doctrine of God's providence. Nineteenth-century revivalists added the consumption of alcohol and smoking because of the dangers of using or abusing these substances. By the end of the nineteenth century, a whole sector of the American church (excluding Catholics and Episcopalians) identified spiritual vitality and commitment to Christ with adherence to this code—or, at least, they tended to deny their existence outside it. In the twentieth century, what had begun as an effort to facilitate inner spiritual freedom became a stumbling block to non-Christians and to many within the church. Ironically, these standards were an obstacle to evangelistic outreach, and a firebreak to block the spread of spiritual renewal within the church.

We can see this same view of worldliness at work within the early church. The Jewish cultic Law, a mixture of health-promoting taboos and symbolic prohibitions, had to be laid aside as a mark of first-class Christian citizenship. If the Jewish Christians had won in their effort to make all Gentiles adopt circumcision and their Law as a part of conversion, not only would the essence of the gospel have been compromised, but there would have been very few Gentiles converted!

Since the Law had been inspired by God and strongly inculcated during the history of Israel, God had to abrogate it by a direct revelation to the apostle Peter (Acts 10:9-48; compare with 11:1-18; 15:1-35). Paul strongly warns against allowing this style of religion into the Messianic kingdom, except as one lifestyle among which Christians may voluntarily choose. Mandating the Law for all would be a great hindrance to mature spiritual growth, as well as to missionary outreach:

> See to it that no one take you captive through hollow and deceptive philosophy, which depends on human tradition and the basic principles [or training codes] of this world rather than on the Messiah. . . . When you were dead in your sins . . . God made you alive with the Messiah. He . . . canceled the written code, with its regulations, that was against us and that stood opposed to us; he took it away, nailing it to the cross. . . . Therefore do not let anyone judge you by what you eat or drink. . . . These are a shadow of the things that were to come; the reality, however, is found in the Messiah. . . . Since you died with the Messiah to the basic principles of this world, why, as though you still belonged to it, do you submit to its rules: "Do not handle! Do not taste! Do not touch!"? These are all destined to perish with use, because they are based on human commands and teachings. Such regulations indeed have an appearance of wisdom, with their self-imposed worship, their false humility and their harsh treatment of the body, but they lack any value in restraining [the indulgence of the flesh]. (Col 2:8, 13-14, 16-17, 20-23 NIV)

The last verse of this passage—note that the NIV perpetuates the typical misunderstanding of "the flesh" as "sensual indulgence"—may also be translated as "These [regulations] . . . are of no value, serving only to indulge the flesh"—that is, religious flesh (Col 2:23

RSV, margin). What is proposed as a way to bridle our carnal natures may actually function as a spur.

Before the Messiah came, Israel needed a God-inspired training code to keep it from being dissolved in the world. But the Messiah has come, liberating God's people from their internal enemies: the law of sin and the legal code designed both to restrain and expose it (see Rom 7:1-12). As he liberates us inwardly from these enemies—and from those other interior enemies identified by Luther, a bad conscience and the fear of death—he also liberates us from oppressive enemies in the world. In this new situation, adherence to cultural codes throws us back into a defensive posture like that of Israel in the Old Testament. It lowers us to thinking like the world, concentrating on law and obedience. But we should be on the offensive to win the world to the Messiah, through the good news of salvation by grace through faith.

Of course believers may want to keep certain habits out of their own behavior because of their upbringing and their preferences. And they certainly will want to avoid shocking others or causing them to stumble in any way, as Paul indicates in Romans 14 and 1 Corinthians 8. Nevertheless, far from being a way to break conformity with the world, codes of outward behavior in indifferent matters are just the sort of thing the world manufactures and takes seriously. They are themselves the essence of worldliness (see Col 2:20)! If we talk grace and faith, but insist that Christians must live partly bound up in a law code, the world will not hear our message clearly. And our own spiritual lives will suffer also, as we revert to the bondage of legalism.

The Puritans gave us another view of worldliness. For them a "worldly" person was anyone absorbed in the love and pursuit of material wealth or pleasure. The modern Christian business leader who observes the fundamentalist do's and don'ts but pursues profit at the expense of workers and the environment would be labeled "worldly" by the Puritans—as would the worker who pursues high wages and a better standard of living without caring for the general good of the commonwealth, or the needs of management, or the needs of other classes and nations. And the preacher who offers faith in Jesus as the key to material wealth or physical health would also be recognized as "worldly."

This definition of "worldliness" seems at first to be in tune with one major biblical passage on the subject: "Do not love the world or anything in the world. If anyone loves the world, the love of the Father is not in him. For everything in the world—the cravings of sinful man, the lust of his eyes and the boasting of what he has and does—comes not from the Father but from the world. The world and its desires pass away, but the man who does the will of God lives forever" (1 Jn 2:15-17 NIV). At first glance, the "worldly" person here would be one who is too much in love with this world, with its beauties or goods or rewards.

The great Augustinian tradition of spirituality identifies "inordinate affection" as one of the main adversaries of spiritual vitality. And there is considerable truth to this. Augustine saw that however beautiful God's creation is, to love and serve it more than God is really to worship the creature rather than the Creator. A heart filled with idolatrous self-love (pride) or love of creatures (sensuality) could not, at the same time, hold the love of God. Loving God and loving others as ourselves would be impossible for such a heart. "Worldliness," then, would simply lie in imitating all humanity's inordinate love of creatures, and in resisting or ignoring the Creator. But even this is not a sufficient definition of "the world."

What the World Is

If we look more closely at 1 John 2:15-17, however, we see that "everything in the world" is identified, not with things or material creatures, but with "the cravings of sinful man, the lust of his eyes and the boasting of what he has and does." These are, however, just manifestations of the *flesh*. They are the desires that motivate fallen humanity.

Nevertheless, these desires create *patterns* or *structures of behavior* which make up the corporate life of fallen humanity; together, they shape the structures of the society in which we live. Capitalists and Communists seek wealth and power and avoid failure and exposure, while professing allegiance to the market system or humankind. Thieves seek goods and avoid prison. People grasp at "what's in it for me" and avoid rebukes or punishments. All these desires and behaviors create systems of interlocking relationships, of conspiracy and confrontation, back scratching and back stabbing. The world becomes a ghastly caricature of what God intended. These relationships keep the machinery of civilization running. But they are nothing like the kingdom of heaven. To be trapped in them forever would be like being damned to the nightmare of hell. But those who respond to the Messiah will not be thus trapped. This world is "passing away" in the dawning of the kingdom. "Because our salvation is nearer now than when we first believed. The night is nearly over; the day is almost here" (Rom 13:11-12 NIV).

The *world* can be defined as *corporate flesh*—a pattern of drives and actions resulting from the interrelationship of all the individual flesh in the bulk of humanity. As human beings design economic systems, governments, businesses, and many lesser structures of civilization, they are influenced partly by reason and God's "common grace" (the grace and wisdom even nonbelievers are granted), and partly by their own selfish interests and carnal natures. The resulting structures are always in some measure crooked. They are like the house in Shirley Jackson's novel *The Haunting of Hill House,* where no single joint was set at a right angle.[1]

The structure of corporate flesh leads individuals into sin in several ways. For one thing, it makes some forms of evil (such as racism and economic oppression) so widespread that they are almost invisible; we find we are supporting them without even knowing it. All white people living in South Africa, for instance, benefit from apartheid, even those who have not deliberately produced it. Those who do not deliberately fight it are in some measure guilty of oppressing Blacks.

The Bible teaches that we are responsible to uncover hidden forms of corporate evil and resist compliance with them: "You shall not follow a multitude to do evil" (Ex 23:2). This is difficult to do. For this reason God raises up leaders as prophets to point out these evils. The prophets, we might add, are not always Christians or religious leaders. God sometimes raises up prophets among unbelievers when the church itself is part of the problem.

Whenever Christianity is infected by the world, it permits the creation of—or even forces into existence—alternate voices pointing to existing evils. Worldliness in the church has cast immense and permanent shadows in history: Islam, secular humanism, Marxism, unbalanced forms of liberalism or conservatism. These in turn cast shadows in the church as it reacts against the imbalance it perceives. Sometimes the church moves to the opposite extreme, or, when it is unable to detect the distortion in these movements, it becomes magnetized by them, made over in their shape, "blown here and there by every wind of teaching" (Eph 4:14 NIV).

The church's mind always exists like a bar of iron in the induction coil of an electric magnet. It is very difficult for it to avoid being destructively shaped and influenced by what goes on in the world, even to the extent of being "conformed to this world" (Rom 12:2). I call this conformity *destructive enculturation*. To defend itself against this conformity, the church often resorts to another form of worldliness, the invention of behavioral taboos. The strategy of attempting to shield ourselves from pollution in a human law code is part of what I call *protective enculturation*.

Scripture uses powerful symbols to present the great destructive force of the world. In the Old Testament the Gentiles are one of these images. Walled off from the nations by its God-given Law, Israel is constantly warned not to contaminate itself by contact with unclean surroundings or with the practices of its neighbors, especially their religious practices.

Even so, by the time of the Messiah's coming, Jewish religious life had been deeply penetrated by the worldliness which can grow up despite (or even because of) protective enculturation. There were in Israel many faithful believers who waited for the Messiah, trembling at the Law and depending earnestly on their sacrifices to cleanse them from guilt. But Pharisaic orthodoxy was full of legalism and disguised idolatries of fame and power: the worldliness of the church.

Outside God's chosen people, the main corrupting power of the world is presented in the biblical symbol of Babel or Babylon, "the great city that rules over the kings of the earth" (Rev 17:18 NIV). This city—Augustine called it "the City of Man"—first appears in Genesis 11, before the calling of Abraham and the development of Israel. At this juncture, "the whole world had one language and a common speech" (Gen 11:1 NIV). This unified body of humanity determined to build "a city, with a tower that reaches to the heavens, so that we may make a name for ourselves and not be scattered over the face of the whole earth" (Gen 11:4 NIV). Evidently this plan held such potential for corruption and cruelty that God directly confused human communication by diversifying language in order to build firebreaks between the various centers of rebellion. But the ground plan of the city of man has always been to regain its original unity and subjugate all the earth to its power.

The successive attempts at establishing world empires all display this impulse, which is a corrupted form of humanity's original mandate to hold dominion over the earth (Gen 1:26). In Daniel 7, the major powers arising in world history (the Babylonian, Assyrian, Macedonian and Roman Empires) are symbolized by great beasts which rise up out of the sea of nations and rule for a while (Dan 7:3-8). Like Frankenstein monsters, these empires are ill made and inevitably disintegrate. But while they stand, they continue reaching out for universal rule. Of course, only the city of God, the kingdom of the Messiah, persists throughout history and for eternity; all other empires perish.

The heart of these empires is hostile toward God and his people. If they could, they would wipe these off the earth. The wheat field of God's kingdom is infested with deadly weeds, which not only take up space but threaten the life of the wheat. Nevertheless, with great patience and mercy, God allows both to grow together, for many of the weeds will end as wheat. The two cities go on together in a perpetual cold war, like the East and West today. Usually they are in an uneasy coexistence; occasionally, in open conflict. The extent of God's mercy toward the members of the fallen world system is displayed in his willingness to spare Sodom, a proud oppressive, dissolute city, if ten righteous persons would be found within it (Gen 18:32). And his heart of love and patience is shown also in Jeremiah's counsel to the Israelites in exile: "Seek the peace and prosperity of the city to which I have carried you into exile. Pray to the LORD for it, because if it prospers, you too will prosper" (Jer 29:7 NIV).

At Pentecost, Babel is reversed, and the kingdom of God expands as a mission of peacemaking and bridge building across linguistic barriers. The result is the city of God, "a great multitude that no one could count, from every nation, tribe, people and language" (Rev 7:9 NIV). So far as the nations do not subject themselves to the Messiah, however, they continue to be under the sway of the world. Revelation 17 presents the most complete and horrifying image of the world in Scripture:

> One of the seven angels . . . said to me, "Come, I will show you the punishment of the great prostitute, who sits on many waters. With her the kings of the earth committed adultery and the inhabitants of the earth were intoxicated with the wine of her adulteries." . . . The woman was dressed in purple and scarlet, and was glittering with gold, precious stones and pearls. She held a golden cup in her hand, filled with abominable things and the filth of her adulteries. This title was written on her forehead:
>
> MYSTERY
> BABYLON THE GREAT
> THE MOTHER OF PROSTITUTES
> AND OF THE ABOMINATIONS OF THE EARTH.
>
> I saw that the woman was drunk with the blood of the saints, the blood of those who bore testimony to Jesus. (Rev 17:1-6 NIV)

The woman is riding on a scarlet beast, representing a coalition of earthly gangs or monarchies ranged against the kingdom of God. "They will make war against the Lamb, but the Lamb will overcome them because he is Lord of lords and King of kings" (Rev 17:14 NIV). This coalition is destined to turn against the woman and "bring her to ruin" (Rev 17:16 NIV). In Revelation 18, this ruin is described as the smashing of all commercial and governmental life that will not submit to God. "Your merchants were the world's great men. By your magic spell all nations were led astray. In her was found the blood of prophets and of the saints, and of all who have been killed on the earth" (Rev 18:23-24 NIV). Capitalists and Communists who read these chapters might identify one another as the guilty party. But the truth is that all of the world systems that are against God and our full humanity are a part of this army.

Discerning the World

Just as flesh is often linked with idolatry, corporate flesh is usually related to the worship of idols. Inordinate affection—loving ourselves or others or things more than God—always bends us out of shape. It also introduces bends and twists into what we build. Necessary seats of power become too powerful. Necessary accumulators of capital accumulate too much. The beautiful and famous live in a dream world of lust and glamor. The world as it exists is full of these twistings and distortions. Nothing exists in its proper proportion. Sometimes fools wear crowns, while true moral or spiritual greatness is powerless or buried in oblivion. Candles are hidden under bushels while dead bulbs are exhibited on lampstands as though they were full of light. Mountains become valleys and valleys become peaks. This is why when John the Baptist came he ministered with Isaiah's words, predicting that the Messiah would straighten out these inequities: "A voice of one calling in the desert, 'Prepare the way for the Lord, make straight paths for him. Every valley shall be filled in, every mountain and hill made low. The crooked roads shall become straight, the rough ways smooth. And all mankind will see God's salvation' " (Lk 3:4-6 NIV).

How the Messianic task of making crooked roads straight and rough ways smooth is to be accomplished will be dealt with in part three. Here we must consider how we are to discern the shape of the world. We are commanded not to "conform any longer to the pattern of this world, but be transformed by the renewing of your mind. Then you will be able to test and approve what God's will is—his good, pleasing and perfect will" (Rom 12:2 NIV). But how are we to avoid conforming to the world if we do not recognize its shape?

The essential mark of the world is *distortion* of created goods and legitimate values. As Paul and Augustine teach, nothing which exists is evil in itself. Otherwise it could not be the creation of a good God. Evil is the privation of good—that is, it is the *twisting* of some good toward an evil end or an improper place in the plan of God. Sin is a "missing of the mark." Humankind is like Atalanta in the Greek fable, who lost a race because she kept veering to the right and left to pick up golden apples which her opponent had placed in view. All human structures reflect these excursions. Usually these crooked places take the form of excesses or depletions, too much or too little.

Thus we legitimately seek after wealth, but often by corrupt means and with uncontrolled zeal toward selfish ends. Mountains of accumulation appear, together with valleys of starvation. The accumulators defend themselves with excuses that there is not enough wealth to go around (Malthus) or that life is a struggle for the survival of the fittest (Darwin). The poor endure their lot or plan revolution, sometimes loosing worse excesses in the wake of their occasional success. As Zoltán Kodály remarked, capitalism is the oppression of man by his fellow man, and communism is the reverse.

We legitimately seek after freedom, for God made us to enjoy at least an analog of his untrammeled liberty. But we in the West turn our freedoms into license, the uncontrolled search for wealth, power and pleasure. As a result, the liberty of many in our society is curtailed, and the Arab world is shocked by our depravity. In the East, on the other hand, is an appearance of sobriety and justice, but all under the pall of an iron constraint. If one side or the other could exhibit both liberty and justice, it could win the allegiance of all the world!

We seek after technological mastery, and this is right, for Adam named the animals and tended the Garden. But the world offers now a landscape of either sorcery or savagery. We have, on the one hand, the Faust-like humanist technicians, who ignore the Creator and abuse his creation. Ironically, we ourselves are setting loose the environmental plagues of the book of Revelation and plotting nightmares of inhuman control (B. F. Skinner, *Walden Two;* C. S. Lewis, *That Hideous Strength;* Aldous Huxley, *Brave New World*). On the other hand, we have the undeveloped countries with their deep need for a humane technology. Technology has given us modern medicine, with its power to heal, and drugs, with their power to destroy. Technology is a blessing, not an ungovernable evil; but its use in the modern world is deeply distorted.

In America, conformity to the world is evident in the style of politics which looks out for "American interests" abroad at the expense of other nations and the general well-being of the human community. It is reflected in a foreign policy which either pursues domination over other countries or disinterested isolation from them.

In our economic life, the distorting presence of the world is present both in the sloth of able persons subsisting on welfare and in the harried activism of those climbing the ladder of success. It is present not only in the sensual irresponsibility of the 1960s counterculture, but also in the straight life the hippies condemned—the traumatic competition of business which destroys workers, executives and their families. Allen Ginsberg summed up the economic shape of the world in the image of the idol Moloch, in whose burning arms Americans sacrifice their children as they compete for success.[2]

In our consumer society, conforming to the world is succumbing to the lure of covetousness induced by advertising and the purchasing of items we do not need. It is businesses and advertising using any technique—especially sex—to sell goods, even if it debases women and creates a dangerous moral environment. It is businesses which are influenced by Christians in management or labor, but which advertise their products on television programs that model and promote non-Christian values. It is conforming to styles which are designed not for beauty, but for planned obsolescence.

Conforming to the world is the various idolatries of the American dream. It is marriages in which spouses are either abused as maidservants or meal tickets, or put on pedestals and idolized. It is family life destroyed by careerism, or careers neglected through a retreat into the family. It is sexuality either uncontrolled or repressed. It is parental permissiveness or authoritarianism. It is unnatural isolation of the individual lost in the secular city, or privacy invaded by technological spies.

Worldly Education

Perhaps the most serious source of conformity to the world is the American system of education. Schools began as nurseries of piety for young Christians. Originally, Harvard was designed above all to produce and reinforce Christian leaders. Colleges and universities founded on this basis have usually decayed rapidly and moved away from their original purpose. This process usually moves through a phase of rationalistic or "liberal" Christianity, leading eventually to religious "neutrality," total ideological pluralism, or consistent commitment to secular humanism.

Pagan humanism is the worst enemy of Christianity confronting us in the modern world. It is no accident that 666, the number of antichrist in Revelation 13:18, is called "man's number." The humanist antichrist has deeply penetrated the American system of public and private education. This began with Jefferson's deistic pluralism. It was further advanced by the agnosticism of Horace Mann and perfected by John Dewey, the pragmatic philosopher of naturalistic humanism. This antichristian religion (for it is nothing less than an alternate system of doctrine, values and meaning opposed to Christianity) has gained control of our teachers' colleges. It has penetrated much of our primary and secondary school systems with antibiblical presuppositions. It has pretended to be neutral, but it has steadily whittled away at religious freedom in our public schools. It has argued that the founders' reluctance to establish any single sect logically leads to a ban on teaching creationism as an alternate theory of the origin of earth and humanity. Under the pretense of defending non-Christian religions, it has attacked all religion.

To find the principal modern antichrist in charge of America's schools is shocking and frightening. No wonder we lose so many children to atheism and agnosticism! No wonder that we find so much conformity to the world within the church! But we must remember that there are sobering reasons why this has happened.

For one thing, Christian parents have been largely indifferent to the secularization of universities, continuing to send their children to deforming institutions out of sentiment, nostalgia, social pride and the desire for good business contacts. Once as I crossed Harvard Yard on my way to a chamber concert at Sanders Hall, a theater which looks as if it once was a church—a fitting emblem for the university—I asked myself, "Why has this happened to Harvard and other schools?" An almost audible voice spoke a verse of Scripture in my heart: "Let not the wise man glory in his wisdom, let not the mighty man glory in his might, let not the rich man glory in his riches; but let him who glories glory in this, that he understands and knows me, that I am the LORD who practice steadfast love, justice, and righteousness in the earth; for in these things I delight, says the LORD" (Jer 9:23-24).

But this verse is a two-edged scalpel. It lays bare the neglect of duty and complicity with evil of generations of administrators, faculty and alumni. It also reveals the dereliction of Christian schools. They have also failed to promote mercy, justice and righteousness in the earth, and so have been less than fair to humanity. Not infrequently they are parochial, isolated purveyors of a smug and sterile culture. No wonder ethical humanism arises to remedy this neglect! As we have said, bad Christianity casts shadows, and some of these God uses to bring his mercy to a humanity which finds itself "folded, spindled and mutilated" by bad religion. Marxism, as many have pointed out, is a Christian heresy with many goals which are essentially biblical. An educational system which does not seek God's agenda will soon find itself opposed by one which does.

For Christians simply to desert or subvert the humanist educational establishment is therefore an oversimplified solution. Reinstituting public prayer or banning value-free sex education will not cure the virus infecting this system. More strategic than abandoning these schools or merely trying to attach a Band-Aid or two would be to convert the systems already in place. We might even work with them in some kind of mutually beneficial pluralism, provided humanists can recognize and back away from their attack on Christian values. Of course, alternative educational systems can produce pressure which forces the establishment to be amenable to persuasion. Ideally, all schools should be Messianic institutions, as Deuteronomy 6 clearly indicates. But it may be dangerous to truth and intelligence to bring about this situation prematurely, before the church has purged itself of the superstition and irrationality which have often driven it to cripple human civilization.

The World in the Church
The church itself, finally, suffers from conformity to the world. In the church two equally distorting extremes have existed side by side: superstition (overbelief) on the one hand, and what I call substition (underbelief) on the other. The early and medieval church erred in the former direction. The church, having set itself in an adversary

position toward Judaism, further alienated itself from its roots by taking on forms of piety which Jews had learned to detest. The animism and polytheism in pagan cultures soon resurfaced in Christianized forms after these cultures were "converted."

Reading Augustine's mockery of the pagan tutelary deities in *The City of God* is instructive. The great theologian points out that a roomful of gods and goddesses in the groom's bedchamber was required just to consummate a marriage! We see these intermediaries reintroduced in the church in the form of saints who are supposed to watch over sailors, automobile safety and lost causes. The Protestant Reformation's contention that praying to the saints gravely insults Christ's role as sole mediator has not yet been adequately heard by the Roman Church. Until it is, Jews and other readers of the Old Testament may stumble and reject the Catholic faith, along with other thoughtful persons who cannot swallow Christianity with pagan admixtures. The Marian devotion, which is in Protestant eyes a dangerous virus among conservative Catholics, must be trimmed back to the legitimate place it had in Irenaeus's concept of the second Eve. Otherwise, Mary herself will not see the nations won to the Messiah by the Roman Catholic Church.

And so there may be a germ of truth in the old Protestant conviction that the millennial state cannot be reached before the destruction of the Roman antichrist. Nevertheless, the Protestant antichrist also needs to be destroyed! Protestant superstition and enculturation have generated a set of diseases worse than Catholic hagiolatry. The worst viruses in modern Catholicism are diseases caught from liberal Protestantism! Perhaps they have been set loose to administer the coup de grâce to the theology of Trent. But they may only generate further conservative reaction. Mainline Protestantism itself is a tragedy when viewed with the eyes of biblical faith. The Western educational system has systematically smashed the Reformers' scriptural foundations, exiling them to a world beyond historical testing, leaving the church with no role in the real world except to supply Christian reasons for seeking humanist goals. Its theology, as James McCord said in the late 1960s, is a shambles.

Idolatries of superstition magnify the glory of the creature at the expense of the Creator. They ascribe worth and mediatorial power to glorified humans and angels, and detract from the mediatorial dignity of the Messiah. Idolatries of substition, on the other hand, also rob God of his glory and the Messiah of his redemptive office, through unbelief in miracles and in the supernatural power and providential control of the biblical God. Denial of the virgin birth is an attack on the glory of the God-man who is the Messiah. Ignoring or demythologizing the cross and resurrection is an attack on his role as mediator. "Liberal" theology, in the strict sense of the word, is bad not just because it divorces faith from history, but also because it is an assault on the character of God.

Fundamentalist, charismatic and evangelical believers who have retained their roots in Scripture are contemptuous of the errors of Catholics and mainline Protestants. But they themselves are victims of distortions which make them a laughingstock to these two other groups and to secular onlookers. Civil religion which wraps the cross in the American flag, television hucksters and celebrity superstars, factions and political divisions worse than the Sanhedrin, a political and economic posture unrelated to the needs of the poor, evangelistic methods which are just religious forms of hard-sell salesmanship, cultic taboos which strangle the rising generations, canonized eccentricities and vagaries of the spirit, heretical doctrines sweeping through congregations like varieties of influenza—these are just a few of the problems in conservative Protestantism.

The major distortions both in the world and in worldly Christianity spring from the perversion of the legitimate human drive for dominion. God made us lord over all other creatures on earth, and every human being naturally desires to be a lord or lady. But God put Adam in the Garden "to till it and keep it" (Gen 2:15)—to service its needs as well as to enjoy the benefits of dominion. The world's pattern of kingly rule is to seek to dominate the world rather than to serve it.

In the church, the drive to gain power is usually disguised somewhat as a desire for fame and approval in order to serve better. Jesus says of the Pharisees, "Everything they do is done for men to see. . . . They love the place of honor at banquets and the most important seats in the synagogues; they love to be greeted in the marketplaces and to have men call them 'Rabbi' " (Mt 23:5-7 NIV). Elsewhere Jesus indicates what is necessary to break this conformity to the world: "You know that the rulers of the Gentiles lord it over them, and their great men exercise authority over them. It shall not be so among you; but whoever would be great among you must be your servant, and whoever would be first among you must be your slave; even as the Son of man came not to be served but to serve, and to give his life as a ransom for many" (Mt 20:25-28).

The antithesis of worldly behavior, and the cure for conformity to the world, is set forth particularly in the "upside-down kingdom" of the Sermon on the Mount. The lifestyle of the kingdom is not proud but poor in spirit, not self-confident but meek and sensitive to conviction of sin, not self-righteous but repentant, not praise-seeking but God-obeying even to the point of suffering persecution, not vengeful but forgiving, not ostentatious or laborious in piety but secretive and simple, not anxious or acquisitive but content in serving God, not judgmental but merciful. If these patterns can be nurtured in the church, they will affect the moral structure of the rest of humanity. Part three will suggest ways this can be done.

Discussion Questions

Recommended supplemental reading: chapter 12 in *Dynamics*. Scripture for meditation: Revelation 18.

1. Has your Christian background taught you to avoid "worldliness"? What has been your understanding of this word?

2. What is the biblical meaning of "the world"?

3. Why are *Babel* and *Babylon* effective symbols for the world?

4. How does the present world system make it difficult for us to lead consistent Christian lives?

5. How does the existence of "common grace" affect our ways of responding to the world?

6. What kinds of "conforming to the world" are most problematic for Christians today?

7. How is the church conforming to the world?

The
Devil

5

Walter Rauschenbusch's portrayal of "the kingdom of evil" touches on many of the points we have covered in our treatment of the world.[1] Rauschenbusch also uncovers many forms of sin which are not ordinarily considered part of the flesh. But he completely neglects the third of the three classical negative dynamics, the devil; he dismisses the subject as leftover "Persian dualism." For the founder of the social gospel, the kingdom opposing the reign of Christ was primarily a conspiracy of bad human beings and bad systems. More recent theologies have not gotten much further. A great deal has been written recently about "principalities and powers," the "superpersonal powers of evil," which only echoes and amplifies Rauschenbusch's reduction of "the devil" to "the world."

This material is helpful to us because it underscores the fact that ideologies and economic and political systems do indeed form a major part of the resistance to the kingdom of Christ, and that these are going to have to be challenged as his reign expands. Like many discoveries of modern scientific humanism, especially in the fields of medicine and psychology, these studies of principalities and powers include valuable insights which would never have occurred to us if we had been content just to blame all the trouble in the world on the powers of darkness, and let it go at that.

Demythologizing Our Doubts

Nevertheless, any treatment of the forces opposing the Messianic kingdom will not be practical or realistic if it overlooks the biblical portrayal of the superhuman, but fully personal, forces that empower and direct evil human beings and systems. This is the message of that supremely practical pastoral theologian, C. S. Lewis, who bluntly refused to discard or reinterpret the devil. Screwtape might be discounted as a piece of allegorical furniture. But *That Hideous Strength* makes it clear that Lewis believed there is diabolical power behind antichristian humanism.[2] The Head of NICE (the National Institute of Coordinated Experiments) only seems to be a disembodied human head sustained technologically. What he really is becomes clear at the end, when the head asks to be worshiped by human sacrifice even though its plug has been pulled.

Why have modern theologians been so reluctant to acknowledge the practical relevance of biblical Satanology? It may not be impertinent to suggest that the devil has had a hand in this. "Hell is a conspiracy," as Whittaker Chambers once said, "and the first requirement of a conspiracy is that it remain underground."[3] If "the god of this world has blinded the minds of the unbelievers, to keep them from seeing the light of the gospel of the glory of the Messiah" (2 Cor 4:4), then he is surely capable of pulling the wool over the eyes of Christian intellectuals and whispering in their ears that he does not exist.

But it is also true that modern folklore and comic literature have trivialized the devil. An imp with a fork in a red union suit is certainly no threat to our spiritual lives or the kingdom of Christ. "The devil made me do it" is so obviously a cop-out that it makes many Christians want to rule any such influence out of bounds. Other literature has domesticated the devil, turning him into a con man easily outwitted by the likes of Daniel Webster. Some horror films have given us visions closer to biblical demonology, but these tend to frighten us. And so when we hear about the powers of darkness, we either smile and dismiss them, or feel creepy and avoid the subject. The reader may be experiencing one of those reactions right now. But let us stick to the subject, for spiritual growth and effective service in the kingdom of God are impossible without it. How far will a gardener get who is embarrassed to talk about bugs?

The great Catholic and Protestant doctors of the spiritual life have always viewed demonology as an eminently practical subject, related both to personal spirituality and to the establishment of the kingdom of Christ. Desert fathers like Anthony went into the wastelands not to retreat from the world but to press the battle on the devil's own ground. Whether or not they were right in drawing these conclusions from Scripture, later traditions of Christian spirituality have refined and purified their emphasis on spiritual warfare. Luther's greatest hymn is a declaration of his intent to exorcise both the church and the world. When he threw an inkwell at the devil, he symbolized his whole career. Protestant Puritans and Counter-Reformation Catholics competed with one another in the production of battle manuals like William Gurnall's *The Christian in Complete Armour* (a best seller which was reprinted many times) and John Downame's *The Christian's Warfare against the World, the Flesh and the Devil.* Bunyan's *Pilgrim's Progress* and *The Holy War* are so full of battle imagery that their spirituality must be incomprehensible to demythologizing modernists. Edwards and the other leaders in the Great Awakening made constant practical references to the forces of darkness, whose rule they were attempting to break.

In the Second Evangelical Awakening and later renewal movements there is less perception of the opposing forces. This is because the West passed through a watershed in the eighteenth century in which superstition was abandoned for the opposite error, substition. The Enlightenment did us a great service by teaching us not to fear a great many enemies which do not exist: witches who really can harm you, vampires, werewolves and many other things which go bump in the night. But it also did some very irrational things: it denied even the existence of witches and attempted to banish from the universe all creatures intermediate between God and man, including angels.

This attempt, as we now know, was just a prelude to banishing God himself, replacing him with natural laws. Modern Christians draw back from this extreme rationalism. But at the same time, they swallow much of what the Enlightenment said about the devil, other major biblical doctrines and the Bible itself. Now the devil, like the hog-nosed snake, has only two basic strategies: he can bluff or he can hide. He can try to terrify us with pretended power, as he did before the Reformation, or, faced with a full proclamation of the victory of Christ, he can go underground.

The Kingdom of Darkness in Scripture

But isn't it plausible that the powers of darkness are an outmoded category, a personification of forces that are now better explained by natural causes? We need to look closely at the data of Scripture to determine whether an impersonal, demythologized view of the kingdom of evil can be squared with the biblical account.

A demonic personality enters the biblical picture at the very outset. Our entrance into sin and spiritual darkness is presented not as a human invention, but as contagion from another species. The personality behind the serpent of Genesis 3 is elsewhere identified as Satan (his name means "the enemy"), also called the devil ("the slanderer"), the leader of a host of fallen angels (created beings above the order of man): "Now war arose in heaven, Michael and his angels fighting against the dragon; and the dragon and his angels fought, but they were defeated and there was no longer any place for them in heaven. And the great dragon was thrown down, that ancient serpent, who is called the Devil and Satan, the deceiver of the whole world—he was thrown down to the earth, and his angels were thrown down with him" (Rev 12:7-9; see also 20:2).

This is no trivial comic figure with a pitchfork, no spook from primitive folklore. It is a superhuman being of great cunning and power, a participant in a cosmic war against the reign of God, in which the Fall of man is only one major skirmish. He is the leader of a host of lesser angels called demons (evil spirits, immaterial personal beings). In effect, the Fall was an invitation to this host of spirits to take up residence in the earth as an occupying army. When Paul speaks of "principalities and powers," he is not talking about abstract systems and forces, but about persons in ruling positions: "Put on the full armor of God so that you can take your stand against the devil's schemes. For our struggle is not against flesh and blood, but against the rulers, against the authorities, against the powers of this dark world and against the spiritual forces of evil in the heavenly realms" (Eph 6:11-12 NIV).

Scripture implies that a demonic power structure exists with different leaders in charge of different areas and nations (Dan 10:21-22). Satan, at the head of these forces, claims to be in control of the fallen world system (Lk 4:6). In fact, Jesus concedes that he is "the prince of this world" (Jn 12:31 NIV). Through our fallen natures, he is able to some degree to direct and control our actions. For he is "the prince of the power of the air, the spirit that is now at work in the children of disobedience" (Eph 2:2). The degree of control is not so great as that of the puppet master over the puppet, but greater than what might be called "immoral suasion." Satan's influence over us is analogous to that of the fisherman who has a fish on the line and who is able to urge and direct the fish's voluntary movements so that it goes where he wants.

The basic motivating drive behind these powers of darkness is their hatred of God, the loyal angelic powers and all other created beings, especially the material creation. Satan is also called *Apollyōn,* "the destroyer" (Rev 9:11). Jesus says that "he was a murderer from the beginning." The terrible distortions and disorders in the present world which conflict with the goodness and harmony of God's original creation are all products of Satan as destroyer (although the devil is so controlled by God's providence that he cannot do anything that does not advance the ultimate purpose of God). Thus the disorders producing disease and psychological illness are indirectly his work. Whatever their intermediate causes, he can directly instigate or aggravate them, as we see from the passages in which Jesus heals by the expulsion of demons (Mt 8:32; 9:33; 15:28; 17:18; compare Job 2:7).

The main motive of the Satanic occupying powers, however, is not simply to torment people and defile the earth. It is to oppose the reign of God. The temptation leading to the Fall is an attack on the joint rulership of the world by God and humanity. When the promise is made that the seed of woman will crush the serpent, all hell is organized to attack that seed. A genocidal attack on Jewish offspring is instigated by the devil, once before the birth of Moses (Ex 1:15-22) and again before the birth of Jesus (Mt 2:13-18). Of course this is also the world and the flesh attacking the Messianic initiative. Pharaoh and Herod resist any incursion on their rule. But this attack, like many others on the people of God, is Satanically engineered.

This is because the agenda of the Messiah and his people is to dislodge and displace the occupying powers of darkness and reverse what they have done. "The Son of God appeared for this purpose, that He might destroy the works of the devil" (1 Jn 3:8 NASB). From Abraham on, the expansion of God's people on the earth has carried on this displacement. Although it has often involved physical conflict, it has ultimately been a spiritual warfare against the occupying powers, waged by an army of liberation. As I have indicated in *Dynamics of Spiritual Life,* the ebb and flow in the life of God's people in times of renewal and decline only reflect the advances and retreats in this invisible warfare, as the territory which is more substantially controlled by God's Spirit expands and contracts.

Thus the devil soon appears on the stage of the New Testament, seeking to subvert Jesus' mission by tempting him to step out of his Messianic role of dependent obedience to his Father (Mt 4:1-11). Jesus detects the hostility of Satan behind the hatred of the Jewish leaders who, like Herod and Pharaoh, do not want their power challenged even by the Messiah (Jn 8:39-47). It is the devil who puts it into the heart of Judas to betray Jesus (Jn 13:2). Finally, Jesus reveals that his death on the cross is nothing else than the ultimate attack of Satan upon his rule, and at the same time the crucial victory which secures his kingdom (Jn 12:31; 14:30).

After the resurrection, the Satanic forces which cannot reach the Messiah must content themselves with resisting the expansion of his kingdom. That resistance is first of all directed at information. The devil would prevent even the mention of the truth about the Messiah, if he could do so. Barring that, Jesus says, "When any one hears the word of the kingdom and does not understand it, the evil one comes and snatches away what is sown in his heart" (Mt 13:19). The devil "has blinded the minds of the unbelievers, to keep them from seeing the light of the gospel of the glory of the Messiah, who is the likeness of God" (2 Cor 4:4).

Beyond simply blocking the message of the gospel, the powers of darkness engage in direct warfare against believers in the Messiah. Peter, who was once told by Jesus that Satan had asked to sift him like wheat (Lk 22:31), warns us that "your enemy the devil prowls around like a roaring lion looking for someone to devour" (1 Pet 5:8 NIV). Paul says that in our daily lives we are continually wrestling against the powers of darkness (Eph 6:12). But the real situation is not simply that we are under attack by Satan, as Jesus was when he was on earth. As we walk in the Spirit, we are actually attacking and destroying the kingdom of evil! Even if the devil kills us physically, as he killed the Messiah, he will only suffer loss as a result. As Revelation says, believers will overcome "him by the blood of the Lamb and by the word of their testimony" (Rev 12:11 NIV).

Any attempt to depersonalize and demythologize this awesome portrayal of cosmic spiritual warfare—to make it refer to the struggles we have with corporations and governments and ideologies—is blatantly trivial and dangerous. Only a literary tin ear could extract this meaning from Scripture. A corporation or an idea will not come after you with the intelligence and malice of a demon. And it will seldom retreat if you command it in the name of Jesus!

The Stratagems of Darkness

What forms do the devil's attacks on Christians take? Let us look briefly at the kinds of problems we encounter in our spiritual lives as a result of Satanic action.

In the medieval period, the major goal of most committed Christians was not to promote the establishment of the Messianic kingdom, but rather to secure the salvation of their own souls, since the doctrine of this period left this issue in doubt. As a result, the ordinary under-standing of the devil's ways of operating against Christians was fairly individualistic. Believers played a sort of king-of-the-mountain game. They achieved holiness by spiritual exercises, while the devil was thought of as circling round them with a pole, seeking to knock them off the heights. Through temptation, he could lead them into mortal sin and even into damnation.

Although they did not believe salvation could be lost, Puritan Prot-estants carried over much of this individualism in their understanding of spiritual conflict. Lacking a developed theology of the kingdom, they had trouble seeing any goal in the devil's dealings with us beyond our own personal affliction.

Given this heritage, most people today think the devil's game plan is limited to temptation. And of course he is called *ho peirazōn*, the tempter (Mt 4:3), with good reason. Nevertheless, temptation is not his most dangerous technique with believers, for they cannot be led away from Christ into damnation.

Still, the temptation of individual believers can cause profound dif-ficulties both in their lives and for the Messianic kingdom. If millions of Christians can be tempted to neglect the church, the Scriptures, prayer and other dynamics of spiritual life, they can be kept at a subsistence level of strength which will offer little threat to the king-dom of evil. If they can be discreetly steered into forms of sin which are in obvious conformity to the world, not only will their own spir-itual lives be weakened, but they will turn others away from the Mes-siah. If teachers and preachers can be tempted to believe and prop-agate falsehood, the fabric of the kingdom will be weakened.

Temptation gains additional power to damage us, however, through another device of Satan: *accusation.* There is no activity which is more characteristic of the devil. Satan is constantly bringing charges against God to us. Meanwhile, at the throne of God, he brings charges against us to God! In Revelation he is called "the accuser of our brethren . . . who accuses them day and night before our God" (12:10). Many of these charges are exaggerated by lies. Remember that the word *dia-bolos* means "slanderer."

Just as easily as he can insinuate temptations into our mind, the devil can tune us in to a kind of demonic mental radio station, which is constantly giving us his opinion of our weakness and depravity. Tokyo and Hanoi found such radio stations helpful in demoralizing opposing troops. The devil is surely not behind them in skill. He can distort our self-image into a caricature with all our faults exaggerated and all our virtues obscured. He can try to destroy our confidence that God loves us, because of continuing patterns of sin in our lives. If we have broken out of those patterns, he can tempt us into individual instances of sin. Then he tries to convince us that sin has us in an unbreakable bondage and that therefore God will neglect or even destroy us in judgment. He can divide us from other Christians by whispering accusations against them in our ears, caricaturing *them* in our minds, perhaps at the same time that he is caricaturing *us* in theirs!

Obviously this sort of bombardment is not the idle work of demons tormenting individual believers. It is a carefully orchestrated effort aimed at strategic targets in the kingdom of God. Dull and half-committed Christians may never experience these things. They are no threat to the powers of darkness and thus draw no fire. But active agents of the kingdom can expect a lifetime of recurring attacks. Cotton Mather remarked that he never attempted anything significant for Christ's kingdom without being buffeted spiritually, either before or after.[4]

All of this involves another characteristic strategy of the devil: *lying*. As Jesus said, "He was a murderer from the beginning, not holding to the truth, for there is no truth in him. When he lies, he speaks his native language, for he is a liar and the father of lies" (Jn 8:44 NIV). Much of this deception is an obvious attempt to divide Christians from one another. If its troops can be turned against one another, the kingdom of God will be stopped dead in its growth.

Most Satanic lies involve malicious misrepresentation or twisting of the facts in ways that darken reputations. However, the devil is also active in brightening the reputations of those who are dangerous to God's kingdom, "for even Satan disguises himself as an angel of light. So it is not strange if his servants also disguise themselves as servants of righteousness" (2 Cor 11:14-15). Thus the demons are the motive power behind false religions, giving their leaders charismatic force and seducing others into following them (1 Tim 4:1; 1 Jn 4:1-3). If we judge from the experience of Peter, the devil can even insinuate his ideas into dedicated Christian believers and make them his mouthpieces on occasion (Mt 16:23). Every part of the church—Catholics and Protestants, fundamentalists and modernists, Western and non-Western—shows some marks of the devil's ability to lead us into believing falsehood, causing us to ignore or doubt biblical truth.

The devil lives in a universe of lies. This is part of the reason his legions are called "powers of darkness." Therefore he works constantly to draw us into the atmosphere of deception. Just as in any efficient dictatorship, the devil seeks to control the media. He seeks to block the broadcast of truth, and to insert and energize whatever is morally degrading and conducive to unbelief.

The devil is not omnipresent. But the Satanic mafia has agents everywhere. The Scripture does not imply that the archdemon himself is constantly prowling around us. But his organization is everywhere. The parts of the earth where the gospel has taken firm root and the church is alive and vigorous are "cleared spaces" in our spiritual jungle. Here, at least, Christians find systems that support them, instead of imperiling their lives and stifling their witness. But there is no place that is wholly free from the presence of fallen angels. Our work is like that of the farmer who must continue to weed the garden at the same time that he strives to drive the jungle back to make more room for cultivation—for the enemy is constantly planting tares within the boundaries of the kingdom (Mt 13:37-39).

The devil is the ultimate oppressor from whose bitter tyranny we all long to be freed. The unjust systems which starve people or enslave their souls are created by human tyrants, but the ultimate designer is Satan. "Theologies of liberation" that deal only with the fallen world system, ignoring our need to be freed from the guilt and power of sin and Satan's oppression, fall desperately short. To topple the power structure created by the interlocking operation of the flesh, the world and the devil, we need a liberator of cosmic dimensions and a Messianic people fully enlightened concerning the difficulty and the supernatural grandeur of the work yet to be done.

Discussion Questions

Recommended supplemental reading: chapter 8 in *Dynamics*. Scripture for meditation: Revelation 12.

   1. How real is the devil to most Christians you have known?

   2. How real is he to you?

   3. How does Scripture depict the devil and his forces?

   4. Which strategies of the devil give you the most trouble?

   5. How is the devil involved in depression and other psychological problems?

   6. Many Christians do not believe in a personal devil. How serious a problem is this for their spiritual lives?

Part III
Dynamics of
Spiritual Life

The Messianic Victory

6

If you are a Christian who has been having trouble remaining spiritually alive—trouble with persistent sins, doubts, fears, depressions and flaws of character—you now understand some of the roots of your problems. Now you know what you have going against you! But here we turn to what you have going for you. In this chapter we will concentrate on the source of victory in our experience—how Jesus conquers the forces of death.

It is both frustrating and depressing to see in our lives the huge catalog of spiritual hurdles and roadblocks we have been reviewing. Our lives are self-centered when they ought to be God-centered. Our sense of the reality of God is intermittent, hit and miss. Often we hide from him in fear. We seem to be attracted to everyone and everything more than we are to God. Most of our interpersonal relations consist of getting things and people properly organized around ourselves, instead of around God. There are many persons toward whom we feel guilty, afraid, angry, jealous or lustful.

On the other hand, our self-concern does not make us any happier about who *we* are. Alone, we are unable to truly love ourselves. We are aware of bad things that we do and good things that we fail to do, and this leaves a sense of guilt. We are occasionally gripped by attitudes that are destructively wrong. And there are years-long bondages of habit that we haven't been able to break. There are areas where other Christians feel we're doing fine, but we know that we're really doing what T. S. Eliot called "the greatest treason: To do the right deed for the wrong reason."[1] If we face the truth, we see that our lives are full of lumps: hills and valleys, excesses and deficiencies. But that's another problem: we don't often want to face the truth, and we are experts at self-deception.

If this picture seems too grim and pessimistic to apply to your life, then either you are far advanced in the Christian life or you had better look again. If it seems all too true and scary and depressing, then take comfort in the fact that you are a normal Christian. Normal Christians do not necessarily always live "the normal Christian life." This is because *the environment* we live in is never normal; it is a state of all-out spiritual war. I often remember the advice of one of my own spiritual mentors: "Remember that it takes *time* to make a saint." One of the greatest Christian leaders in Latin America invites his parishioners into his home so they will see his *faults,* not his saintliness, and be encouraged.

But the picture we have reviewed contains far more than individual faults. We have invited supernatural powers into our world to turn it into a nightmare. These forces have twisted everything into a caricature of the life God intended. They have erected power structures which oppress humanity spiritually as well as materially and socially.

This kingdom of evil resists all efforts at real progress or improvement. The best efforts at forming righteous governments fail because there is no one we can trust to "watch the watchmen." When we get maximum production, there is unjust distribution. When we organize to gain maximum distribution, production lags or freedom is stifled. Nothing works!—because there are no governing hands upon our systems but our own, and those are soiled.

At the end of William Golding's *Lord of the Flies,* the young hero is saved from death at the hands of his companions, former choirboys, by the forces of law and order: the crew from a warship designed to kill men from rival nations.[2] This says it all. The very powers which keep us from killing one another are not angelic. They are ultimately part of systems which are engaged in the planetary equivalent of gang fights. "The whole world," as the apostle says, "is in the power of the evil one" (1 Jn 5:19) and filled with his darkness and lies.

But these difficulties are not the world's most serious problem. Fallen creation is estranged from the holiness of its Creator. It lies under his judgment and curse. The wages of sin, the Scripture reminds us, is death.

We do not like viewing the magnitude of these problems. Once we see them, it is natural for us to want practical answers which will begin working immediately to reassure us that we can stay on top. But there are more important things at stake here than our inner well-being. We are all part of a drama in which the glory of God is being displayed— especially the honor and excellence of his Son. This is why we have taken such a detailed look at the difficulty of redemption. Healing a hard case brings honor to a physician. Defeating a terrible enemy shows the strength of a warrior. The ruin of this world shows the depth and tenacity of God's love, and the grandeur of his Son's achievement.

And so it is essential for us to look entirely outside ourselves to see the splendor of God's plan of deliverance. Salvation is not so much a matter of doing as of *appreciating what God has done.* God wants us to be free from thinking about ourselves long enough to consider what his love has done. After all, to be fully reassured, to be free from the suspicion that we are fooling ourselves and working up faith in nothing more substantial than our own wishful thinking, we need to have our attention fixed on Jesus the Messiah. Our subjective assurance will not be strong unless it is focused on great objective realities.

At the beginning of my Christian life, when I was still nervous and unsure about my relationship with God, I remember driving across one of the great bridges of America. I was looking at the strength of the pylons and the cables, and in my mind I saw a picture of the greater bridge that Jesus has made between a fallen world and God's perfect holiness. In the back of my mind, under all the doubts and fears, a voice said firmly, "The Bridge will hold."

Jesus Our Prophet

God promised that a human leader, a man born of woman, would crush the serpent's head and repair the damage of the Fall (Gen 3:15). The people of God under the Old Covenant experienced deliverance under three kinds of leaders: prophets, priests and kings. When Jesus came, he fully realized these categories in his earthly ministry.

The first great leader whose coming directly prefigures that of Jesus is a prophet, a forthteller who expresses God's mind and will to humanity. Moses is a man of exceptional meekness (Num 12:3), who at one point so identifies with his people that he is willing to be stricken from God's book of life if their sin is not forgiven (Ex 32:32). Nevertheless, there are clear differences between this prophet's ministry and that of Jesus. Moses' miracles are largely destructive judgments, typifying God's use of providential evils to bring us to repentance— just as Moses' Law is used to bring us to the edge of grace. Patient as he is, Moses ultimately expresses anger against God's people (Num 20:6-12). Partly because of this, he is forbidden to lead them into the Promised Land. This task falls to Joshua, whose name is simply the Hebrew form of Jesus, which means "Jehovah saves."

Nevertheless, Moses promises, "God will raise up for you a prophet like me from among you" (Deut 18:15). The great series of prophets from Moses to John the Baptist continued the task of exposing sin and pointing toward grace. When Jesus begins his prophetic ministry, the unprecedented outbreak of miraculous power in healing sickness, casting out demonic powers and raising the dead, declares God's grace in restoring fallen creation, just as the plagues of Egypt declared God's judgment on sin. Jesus conveys these gifts almost recklessly, without demanding immediate doctrinal or moral perfection, but only personal trust in him and his power to deliver.

The overwhelming display of God's mercy toward sinners in these miracles should not obscure the fact that Jesus is by no means the tame figure that current fads and Sunday-school literature have made of him. When I first read the Gospels, I was sobered and scared by the prophetic demands of Jesus: "Unless your righteousness exceeds that of the scribes and Pharisees, you will never enter the kingdom of heaven" (Mt 5:20). My righteousness did not exceed that of anyone I knew, let alone that of the Pharisees, who were the Puritans of their time!

The Ten Commandments seem to call only for a restraint of the worst outbreaks of sin. But Jesus was calling for a revolution in human nature—loving enemies, seeking service rather than power, and adding to right actions a humanly impossible purity of heart. While Jesus never loosed a plague on his adversaries, he did express deep anger against the religious establishment (Mt 23). He twice invaded the temple to attack its leaders physically and overturn its furniture (Jn 2:13-17; Mt 21:12-13).

But Jesus' attacks on religious corruption and pretension are in strong contrast to his mercy and gentleness in dealing with forms of sin which are publicly disreputable. One of the things which aroused the hostility of orthodox onlookers was his public association with moral and religious outcasts. The self-centered religion of his critics invested its energy in building spiritual facades to appease their consciences or attract admiration. Jesus was concerned rather to minister to human need, and to go where there was a sense of sin instead of a false righteousness.

Open idolatry and gross immorality had been the targets of earlier prophets. Jesus is dealing with a different situation: religion has cleaned up its act, masking its basic self-centeredness with orthodoxy and respectability. Against the religious leadership which had all mysteries figured out and the road to righteousness carefully mapped, Jesus delighted to talk in conundrums and violate conventional morality.

This does not mean that he failed to demand moral behavior in obedience to the will of God. Still, his reprimands to the disciples are directed toward their lack of faith and deep spiritual understanding. Coming up against the moral and doctrinal refinements of a religious civilization, Jesus' main task as prophet is to point beyond "the form of religion" (2 Tim 3:5) to the Messianic era. In that age people will be reborn by the Spirit, will understand the kingdom of God (Jn 3:3), and will have its principles written on their hearts instead of locked up in teachers and texts (Jer 31:33).

Jesus Our Priest

After raising up the first prophet, God next established the priesthood, which began with Moses' brother Aaron. In order to balance Moses' clear articulation of the Law, which brings conviction of sin, with the assurance of forgiveness, God regularized a variety of sacrificial offerings. These reminded Israel that although the penalty of sin is death, God can transfer that penalty from us to others if he chooses.

While the Gospels begin with a stress on Jesus' kingship and his earliest teaching centers on the kingdom of God, John the Baptist recognizes Jesus with the words, "Behold, the Lamb of God, who takes away the sin of the world!" (Jn 1:29). In a most remarkable way, Jesus sums up the Old Testament tradition of law and sacrifices by being himself both the priest and the sacrificial victim. He took on himself the penalty of death for sin, which God transferred to him from all those who believe in him.

Modern liberal Protestantism and the several forms of Judaism which strongly resemble it have such a secure sense of righteousness that they have dispensed with priests and sacrifices. The critical reconstruction of the Old Testament which has prevailed in mainline Protestant circles since the nineteenth century holds that priestly religion is inferior to the prophetic spirituality that grew out of it as it gained ethical sensitivity. Protestant liberalism, all the way from its Sunday-school literature to its public acts and proclamations, has an admirable preference for public justice over private spiritual egoism. But it is out of touch with its own underlying sense of guilt. And it ignores the strong witness of the Old and New Testaments with respect to the Messianic priesthood.

The Old Testament is relatively silent about the priestly character of the Messiah. If it had been clearer, the powers of darkness would not have cooperated in his crucifixion. But one clear text indicates that the Messianic king is also to be a priest: "Here is the man whose name is the Branch, and he will branch out from his place. . . . It is he who will build the temple of the LORD, and he will be clothed with majesty and will sit and rule on his throne. And he will be a priest on his throne" (Zech 6:12-13 NIV). Other Old Testament evidence supports the idea that this priest-king is not only to be a priest, but a sacrificial victim:

My God, my God, why hast thou forsaken me? . . .
All who see me mock at me,
    they make mouths at me, they wag their heads;
"He committed his cause to the LORD; let him deliver him." . . .
    They have pierced my hands and feet. . . .
They divide my garments among them,
    and for my raiment they cast lots. . . .
[God] has not despised or abhorred
    the affliction of the afflicted;
and he has not hid his face from him,
    but has heard, when he cried to him. . . .
All the ends of the earth shall remember
    and turn to the LORD;
and all the families of the nations
    shall worship before him. (Ps 22:1, 7-8, 16, 18, 24, 27; see also
    Gen 3:15; Dan 9:26; Zech 12:10)

Perhaps the clearest foreshadowing of Jesus' role as priest and sacrifice is found in one of the suffering servant passages in Isaiah:

He had no beauty or majesty to attract us to him,
    nothing in his appearance that we should desire him.
He was despised and rejected by men,
    a man of sorrows, and familiar with suffering. . . .
Surely he took up our infirmities
    and carried our sorrows,
yet we considered him stricken by God,
    smitten by him, and afflicted.
But he was pierced for our transgressions,
    he was crushed for our iniquities;
the punishment that brought us peace was upon him,
    and by his wounds we are healed.

We all, like sheep, have gone astray,
    each of us has turned to his own way;
and the LORD has laid on him
    the iniquity of us all.
He was oppressed and afflicted,
    yet he did not open his mouth;
he was led like a lamb to the slaughter. . . .
By oppression and judgment he was taken away. . . .
For he was cut off from the land of the living;
    for the transgression of my people he was stricken.
He was assigned a grave with the wicked,
    and with the rich in his death,
though he had done no violence,
    nor was any deceit in his mouth.
Yet it was the LORD's will to crush him and cause him to suffer,
    and though the LORD makes his life a guilt offering,
he will see his offspring and prolong his days. . . .
After the suffering of his soul,
    he will see the light of life and be satisfied;
by his knowledge my righteous servant will justify many,
    and he will bear their iniquities. . . .
For he bore the sin of many,
    and made intercession for the transgressors. (Is 53:2-12 NIV)

The setting of this passage, the great "servant songs" of Isaiah 44—
53, seems at first to be speaking of Israel as a whole. Certainly the
earlier chapters in this series refer to the people of God. But here it
clearly focuses on one individual. This change in focus is consistent
with the Old Testament's view of Israel's failure to obey God. The
good news of the New Testament is that the task which the Israelites
failed at was accomplished by one man in their stead. He lived the
life they could not live . . . and died the death they could not die
without perishing eternally.

Because the Messiah had to be a fitting sacrifice for human sin, he
had to be a man. Now, as the great High Priest intercedes for God's
people, we can be assured that "we have not a high priest who is
unable to sympathize with our weaknesses, but one who in every

respect has been tempted as we are, yet without sin" (Heb 4:15). Thus we can "with confidence draw near to the throne of grace, that we may receive mercy and find grace to help in time of need" (Heb 4:16).

The use of the word *priest* to refer to pastors in the church originated in the writings of the church father Cyprian and so passed into the Catholic, Orthodox and Episcopal traditions. But this is an institutional use of the term, which obscures the fulfillment of the priesthood in Jesus the Messiah. This can have important negative effects on the people of God: an exaggerated deference to clergy and a shirking of the role all Christians have of being "a royal priesthood" (1 Pet 2:9). It can also undermine the laity's assurance of their acceptance with God. The letter to Hebrews expresses God's concern that we fix all our longing for priests and sacrifice on Jesus and his finished work:

> The former priests were many in number, because they were prevented by death from continuing in office; but he holds his priesthood permanently, because he continues for ever. Consequently he is able for all time to save those who draw near to God through him, since he always lives to make intercession for them. For it was fitting that we should have such a high priest, holy, blameless, unstained, separated from sinners, exalted above the heavens. He has no need, like those high priests, to offer sacrifices daily, first for his own sins and then for those of the people; he did this once for all when he offered up himself. (Heb 7:23-27)

The continuing priesthood of Jesus is the source of our assurance and hope: "If God is for us, who can be against us? . . . Who will bring any charge against those whom God has chosen? It is God who justifies. Who is he that condemns? Christ Jesus, who died—more than that, who was raised to life—is at the right hand of God and is also interceding for us. Who shall separate us from the love of Christ?" (Rom 8:31-35 NIV).

Jesus Our King
Ultimate deliverance for Israel was not promised either through prophets or priests, but only through the coming of the Messiah, the anointed king. Just as Protestant liberals and most segments of Ju-

daism are very quiet about priests and sacrifices, they have little to say also about the Messiah. Late nineteenth-century liberalism had almost persuaded itself that behind the Gospel portraits of Jesus lay "the historical Jesus," who was really a social reformer. Then Albert Schweitzer and others established that the only Jesus who could have existed was one convinced that he was the Messiah.

According to the Torah (the first five books of the Old Testament), the Messiah is to be a descendant of the particular Jewish tribe of Judah: "The scepter will not depart from Judah, nor the ruler's staff from between his feet, until he comes to whom it belongs and the obedience of the nations is his" (Gen 49:10 NIV). It is from this tribe that the great King David emerges, "a man after God's own heart."

As we have seen, when David had established his kingdom and proposed to build a permanent dwelling for God in the form of a temple, God reminded him that he had never requested a house to live in, and then said: "I declare to you that the LORD will build a house for you. . . . I will raise up . . . one of your own sons, and I will establish his kingdom. He is the one who will build a house for me. . . . I will be his father, and he will be my son. I will never take my love away from him, as I took it away from your predecessor. I will set him over my house and my kingdom forever; his throne will be established forever" (1 Chron 17:10-14 NIV).

"The son of David" is thus a biblical phrase referring to the Messiah. David's son Solomon built the temple and enjoyed a reign of unprecedented peace and prosperity. His name and glory reflect the peace and splendor of the coming Messianic reign. But clearly God's promise in this passage (which is called "the Davidic covenant") refers to a descendant of David who will be eternal. Matthew and Luke begin their Gospels with genealogies which make it clear that Jesus is this descendant.

"The Son of man" is another phrase referring to the Messiah, deriving from Daniel 7:13-14: "And there before me was one like a son of man, coming with the clouds of heaven. He approached the Ancient of Days and was led into his presence. He was given authority, glory and sovereign power; all peoples, nations and men of every language worshiped him. His dominion is an everlasting dominion that will not pass away, and his kingdom is one that will never be destroyed" (NIV).

According to Nebuchadnezzar's vision recorded in Daniel 2:31-45, the Messiah's kingdom will shatter and supplant all other kingdoms and will last forever. Nations (tribal units with a common ancestry) will continue to exist in submission to the Messianic king, but there will be only one *kingdom,* in which the ruling partnership of man and God will be restored and all creation will be blessed. The Messiah's rule will be shared by the people of God, for the kingdoms "shall be given to the people of the saints of the Most High" (Dan 7:27).

Descriptions of the struggle for the establishment of the Messiah's rule mix images of war with those of a great wedding party in which the conquered nations will partake (Ps 45). Images of war and peace crowd on one another as if the two were somehow identical, as if the conquest of nations were to be accomplished not through weapons but through the outpouring of blessings. The Messiah struggles particularly with rulers, the gang leaders of the rebellious tribes, but they may voluntarily surrender (Ps 2).

In texts referring to the coming king we begin to catch the hint that he is the Son of God as well as the Son of man. "Therefore the Lord himself will give you a sign: The virgin will be with child and will give birth to a son, and will call him Immanuel," that is, "God with us" (Is 7:14 NIV). The image of the Messiah in Isaiah 9 assumes superhuman proportions:

For to us a child is born,
>to us a son is given,
>and the government will be on his shoulders.

And he will be called
>Wonderful Counselor, Mighty God,
>Everlasting Father, Prince of Peace. (9:6 NIV)

The reign of the Messiah is described as a state of extraordinary prosperity, like the reign of Solomon (Amos 9:13-15). And like Solomon's, the Messiah's reign will be one of peace: "They will beat their swords into plowshares and their spears into pruning hooks. Nation will not take up sword against nation, nor will they train for war anymore" (Mic 4:3 NIV).

Above all, his reign will be one of *justice* in government, especially for the poor and oppressed:

Give the king thy justice, O God. . . .
May he judge thy people with righteousness,
    and thy poor with justice! . . .
May he defend the cause of the poor of the people,
    give deliverance to the needy,
    and crush the oppressor! (Ps 72:1-2, 4)

Through the Messiah's rule, the earth will return to the harmony and unhindered knowledge of God that characterized the Garden before the Fall:

The wolf shall dwell with the lamb,
    and the leopard shall lie down with the kid,
and the calf and the lion and the fatling together,
    and a little child shall lead them. . . .
They shall not hurt or destroy
    in all my holy mountain;
for the earth shall be full of the knowledge of the LORD
    as the waters cover the sea. (Is 11:6, 9)

These descriptions of the Messiah's reign are usually stripped of their practical implications by viewing them as only descriptions of the eternal state, the other side of ordinary history. It has been easy during the course of the church's history to use this as an excuse for the continuing social injustice among "Christianized" nations. The Messianic kingdom, it is said, will not be realized in full measure until Jesus returns personally and visibly to set it up, after all the nations are evangelized. But Jesus uses a Messianic prophecy from Isaiah dealing with social justice to signal the thrust of his own ministry: "The Spirit of the Lord is upon me, because he has anointed me to preach good news to the poor. He has sent me to proclaim release to the captives and recovering of sight to the blind, to set at liberty those who are oppressed, to proclaim the acceptable year of the Lord" (Lk 4:18-19).

It is perilously easy to turn this into a pure agenda for social amelioration, as Protestant and Catholic liberals often do. Obviously the text is drained of its meaning if it is isolated from the proclamation of free forgiveness of sins, freedom from the bondage of the flesh and the oppression of Satan. But it is equally perilous to say that the text is devoid of any political or economic implications during the era when the good news is being spread.

When I first became a Christian, the Jewish roommate whose life had convinced me, as an atheist, that there was such a thing as moral righteousness, drew back from the way I had taken. "We Jews say," he remarked, "The Messiah has come? So what has changed? The world is still in the same mess, and the Messiah has come?"

It is easy to say that this is an evasion. And of course it is a defense mechanism. But Jews and others concerned for human justice have a right to ask why the creation of the Christian church, supposedly a Messianic people, has not led to greater transformations in the way things are. To understand this, we need to look more closely at one more role which Jesus played as Messiah.

Jesus the Second Adam

Many of us unconsciously subscribe to the "heroic theory of history." We believe that history is changed by the entrance of heroes—great leaders, prophets, priests and especially kings or presidents. Scripture confirms this belief. God deals with nations and peoples on the basis of their leaders, who in some mysterious way represent the people, express their mind and heart, and bring good or ill on the community by their actions. But the interconnection runs the other way, also. God sometimes gives a nation or a church the kind of leaders it deserves! Or, in a democracy, there may be a connection between the spiritual center of gravity in a people and the kind of leaders they choose to follow.

In any case, the message of Scripture is that if human beings *always* got the leaders they deserve, we would always be represented by tyrants and scoundrels. This is because of the connection between all human beings and the first man, Adam, who represents us all. He has communicated to all humanity a legacy of guilt and lethal punishment. As Paul says, "Because of one man's trespass, death reigned" (Rom 5:17), for "in Adam all die." Even those who have not committed Adam's sin (such as infants) must die physically because of Adam's choice (Rom 5:12-14). Beyond this, however, all men died *spiritually* in Adam, so that all are born "alienated from the life of God" (Eph 4:18). The first Adam has communicated to the hearts of all his descendants an irresistible gravity toward sin. None of us naturally seeks to obey God; instead, we live "in the passions of our flesh, following the desires of body and mind" (Eph 2:3).

But the good news of Scripture is that God has set about creating a whole new humanity in his Son. For Jesus the Messianic King is also the second Adam. The same Jesus who is the *logos* of God—the divine Word expressing God's nature, at once the architect and the blueprint of all creation, who "reflects the glory of God and bears the very stamp of his nature, upholding the universe by his word of power" (Heb 1:3)—was also born of a woman. He was united with humanity in the Incarnation, not only to bear the *guilt* of human sin in a sacrifice which satisfied divine justice, but also to break the *power* of sin in human nature through his death. "For as in Adam all die, so also in the Messiah shall all be made alive" (1 Cor 15:22). This is because there was a mysterious unity between Jesus and all believers when he died on the cross and was raised from the dead (Rom 6:2-7). Our union with the Messiah is the reason those who believe in him are freed from the compulsive power of sin: "Our old self was crucified with him so that the body of sin might be rendered powerless, that we should no longer be slaves to sin—because anyone who has died has been freed from sin" (Rom 6:6-7 NIV).

In the crucifixion, therefore, the old nature and the bent and broken world of fallen humanity went down into the grave. And when Jesus, the second Adam, was raised from the dead, with him rose a new humanity no longer crippled with the curse inflicted on Adam and his descendants: "The creation waits in eager expectation for the children of God to be revealed. For the creation was subjected to frustration, not by its own choice, but by the will of the one who subjected it, in hope that the creation itself will be liberated from its bondage to decay and brought into the glorious freedom of the children of God" (Rom 8:19-21 NIV).

Thus when Jesus rose from the dead, a whole new world rose with him. The Messianic kingdom stretches far beyond Israel's expectations. It is cosmic in scope. In the Messiah, God has "delivered us from the dominion of darkness and transferred us to the kingdom of his beloved Son, in whom we have redemption, the forgiveness of sins" (Col 1:13-14). The realm of his victory extends over the church and far beyond it. "He is the head of the body, the church; he is the beginning and the firstborn from among the dead, so that in everything he might have the supremacy. For God was pleased to have all his fullness dwell in him, and through him to reconcile to himself all things, whether things on earth or things in heaven, by making peace through his blood, shed on the cross" (Col 1:18-20 NIV).

Thus in Jesus' death and resurrection, all the "dynamics of spiritual death" were disarmed and destroyed. Our distance from God and apathy toward him, our compulsive egoism, our selfish manipulation of others, our crippling attitudes and habits, all the shackles of our flesh are dissolved and released. "Therefore, if any one is in Christ, he is a new creation; the old has passed away, behold, the new has come" (2 Cor 5:17). Furthermore, the world itself is open to being renewed in the Messiah, with all its crooked structures straightened and its fields of evil neutralized. For "God was reconciling the world to himself in the Messiah, not counting men's sins against them" (2 Cor 5:19 NIV).

At the deepest level, the oppressive rule of the occupying powers of darkness is broken. "Since the children have flesh and blood, he too shared in their humanity so that by his death he might destroy him who holds the power of death—that is, the devil—and free those who all their lives were held in slavery by their fear of death" (Heb 2:14-15 NIV). Jesus was conscious that his ministry was the inauguration of the Messianic kingdom and that this meant the destruction of the realm of darkness. He tells the disciples, "Behold, I have given you authority to tread upon serpents and scorpions, and over all the power of the enemy" (Lk 10:19). After his death and resurrection, Paul said that "having disarmed the powers and authorities, [Jesus] made a public spectacle of them, triumphing over them by the cross" (Col 2:15 NIV). And John says, "The reason the Son of God appeared was to destroy the works of the devil" (1 Jn 3:8).

If the Messianic victory against the dynamics of spiritual death has been so effective, comprehensive and complete, why do we still experience these negative elements in our lives? The answer, on the individual level, is that the benefits of the Messiah's death and resurrection must be applied in our lives by the Holy Spirit. This application takes place as we respond in *faith.* Jesus himself could not do many mighty works in his home region because of the unbelief there. Thus he is unlikely to work in our lives except as the deep root of unbelief is put to death and replaced by vigorous responses of faith.

We need to turn now to see how we experience the dynamics of spiritual life flowing from our union with the Messianic Victor. But as we turn to our personal lives, we must not take our eyes off Jesus and his kingdom. The first chapter of John's Revelation gives us an image of the powerful presence of Jesus in the midst of his people, standing by the lampstands of his churches and holding their leaders in his hand.

> I saw seven golden lampstands, and among the lampstands was someone "like a son of man," dressed in a robe reaching down to his feet and with a golden sash around his chest. His head and hair were white like wool, as white as snow, and his eyes were like blazing fire. His feet were like bronze glowing in a furnace, and his voice was like the sound of rushing waters. In his right hand he held seven stars, and out of his mouth came a sharp double-edged sword. His face was like the sun shining in all its brilliance.
>
> When I saw him, I fell at his feet as though dead. Then he placed his right hand on me and said: "Do not be afraid. I am the First and the Last. I am the Living One; I was dead, and behold I am alive for ever and ever! And I hold the keys of death and Hades." (Rev 1:12-18 NIV)

Remember that the weapons and the strength of this figure are not directed against us. *They are aimed at our enemies.* When your life seems filled with unbelief and other forms of sin and weakness, get your eyes off yourself and fix them on the Messianic Victor, who once and for all has defeated the flesh, the world and the devil.

Discussion Questions

Recommended supplemental reading: chapter 2 in *Dynamics.* Scripture for meditation: Revelation 1.

1. Why did God establish *prophets* in Israel? How did Jesus occupy the office of prophet? How does he still occupy it today?

2. What was the function of *priests* under the Old Covenant? Why is there no class of priests in the New Testament church? Is there still a place for a human priesthood?

3. Why does God reprove the Israelites at one point for wanting a king (see 1 Sam 8)? Why does he then provide them with a line of kings? How does Jesus exercise his kingship today?

4. Why is Christ's role as *second Adam* so crucially important for us to understand?

5. Scripture speaks of Jesus as the head of a new humanity and the one in whom the entire universe is redeemed and unified. How much have you heard about these aspects of his work? Why are they neglected?

Dynamics of
Individual
Renewal

7

Drawn by the vision of a life centered on God and his kingdom, but confronting the formidable obstacles of the flesh, the world and the devil, we are likely in our human nature to turn first to works. Something within us says that being spiritual is going to be *expensive*. It is at least going to cost us a lot of effort and will power. We think that if Buddhist monks and Hindu gurus have given up ordinary lifestyles for ascetic self-denial, surely Christians must do as much. Jesus said that if we are to enter his kingdom, we must outdo the Pharisees in righteousness (Mt 5:20). Yet the Pharisees tithed even the herbs in their gardens, and they even criticized the disciples for not practicing greater ascetic holiness.

But they criticized Jesus in the same way, and this gives us pause. There must have been something about their "righteousness" which was out of step with Jesus. Paul says that their attempts to be spiritual were what led them to join in the crucifixion of the Son of God and to persecute Christians to the death: "They have a zeal for God, but it is not enlightened. For, being ignorant of the righteousness that comes from God, and seeking to establish their own, they did not submit to God's righteousness. For the Messiah is the end of the law, that every one who has faith may be justified" (Rom 10:2-4).

What is wrong with this kind of spirituality? It is not *enlightened*. It does not spring from a vision of our great weakness and the enormity of our debt of sin. Instead, it is based on confidence in our moral strength and standing. It does not *receive* through faith in the Messiah. Instead, it *achieves* through effort and will power.

Roman Catholics used to assume that ordinary Christians might be good—might do what God expected of them—but that only the exceptionally holy, those who did more than God commanded, could be deeply spiritual. "The spiritual life" was primarily the life of cloistered asceticism.

The New Testament knows nothing of this double standard. It speaks of only one grade of "saint," which includes every Christian believer. Jesus said, "When you have done all that is commanded you, say, 'We are unworthy servants; we have only done what was our duty' " (Lk 17:10). The Christian who "invents" good works or ascetic practices apart from the ordinary path of obedience to God's Word and Spirit, listening for the ring of a heavenly cash register of merits, is building on illusion. In the same way, the liberal Protestant who thinks and acts and votes out of a proper concern for justice, but does so with a hidden pride of achievement, with no awareness of the depth of sin, will be spiritually cold and hard.

But there is also an evangelical spirituality of achievement, as P. T. Forsyth points out. This kind of piety suffers from "an absence of true humility. In its stead there may be either a laboured counterfeit, as painfully sincere as it is simple; or there is a precise self-righteousness which cannot veil a quiet air of superiority." Behind this lack of humility is the claim to a higher level of spirituality and moral achievement, which can only be maintained if the claimant is somewhat in the dark about sin. "This perfectionism is too individualist to feel how the single soul is tainted with the sin . . . of the race. And with all its introspection, it is too unpsychological to realize how the traces of sin live on in the sin-tainted will. . . . In its choicer forms this pietism is devoted to love and prayer; but it seldom escapes the tinge of self-consciousness."[1] "A man may put away many sins, and cultivate no small devotion, and yet be a loveless self-seeker. . . . There are certain forms of self-edification which run out into self-absorption, and leave men . . . working at goodness rather than duty."[2]

Faith and the Primary Elements of Renewal

Forsyth goes on to say that the root of all valid spirituality is faith. "It is a fatal mistake to think of holiness as a possession which we have distinct from our faith. . . . Every Christian experience is an experience of faith; that is, it is an experience of what we have not. . . . It is not our experience of holiness that makes us believe in the Holy Ghost. It is a matter of faith that we are God's children; there is plenty of experience in us against it. . . . The height of sinlessness means the deepest sense of sin."[3]

In all his preaching of the kingdom of God, Jesus did not look for moral achievements in his followers, but for faith in himself. Clearly he regarded Messianic faith as the key to spiritual growth. Paul has the same assessment. He resists the Galatians' effort to add to faith a calculus of legal obedience as a new source of Christian maturity: "Did you receive the Spirit by observing the law, or by believing what you heard? Are you so foolish? After beginning with the Spirit, are you now trying to attain your goal by human effort? . . . Does God give you his Spirit and work miracles among you because you observe the law, or because you believe what you heard?" (Gal 3:2-5 NIV).

Why is faith such a crucial instrument in freeing our lives from the flesh, the world and the devil? We can understand this better if we look again at the damage that has been done to human nature in the Fall. As we have seen, the central core of sin in our personalities is not pride or sensuality but unbelief. Before yielding to the temptation to become independent from God, Eve submitted to a darkening of her mind concerning the glory and goodness of God. This darkness is now the natural condition of all human minds until they are illuminated by faith. Through this central darkness of unbelief in God, the world and the devil are able to crowd in on and control fallen human nature: "The god of this world has blinded the minds of the unbelievers, to keep them from seeing the light of the gospel of the glory of Christ, who is the likeness of God" (2 Cor 4:4).

Patients tested for glaucoma are shown a circle which represents their visual field and then asked to point out the areas they can see. The disease typically darkens the center of the field, while leaving some vision on the periphery. The fallen mind's view of the world is like that of a glaucoma patient. Its view of all things is darkened and distorted by sin, but it has a sort of twilight vision of the periphery of life. In the inner circle of ultimate concerns, however, it is in deeper darkness. It has at best only a dim apprehension of the grandeur of God, the depth of its own need, and the real significance of its relationships to other people. (See appendix A, figure 1.)

The gift of faith is a divine healing of this central blindness of the soul. It is an exact reversal of the entrance into darkness which was the essence of the Fall. Through faith in the Messiah, the soul is able to face reality again with cleared vision. As T. S. Eliot said, "Humankind cannot bear very much reality."[4] But through the light shed by the Holy Spirit on the Messiah and his saving work, the soul can take in at a glance the truth about its own standing before God. It can bear the bad news about the justice of God and the depth of its sin, because it can see in the same glance the good news of the grace of Christ available simply through faith. (See appendix A, figure 2.)

In the blaze of this illumination, faith necessarily involves repentance. The Greek word for repentance, *metanoia*, literally means "a change of mind"—toward God, toward oneself and toward others. It is a Copernican revolution in which self is evicted from the center of life, and the Messiah is enthroned instead. Sorrow for sin and gratitude for the amazing mercy of God replace self-assertion, evasion of God and the soul's fallen motives. Optimum spiritual health simply involves remaining in the focused light of truth concerning our needs and their fulfillment in Jesus' redemptive work (1 Jn 1:5-7). An honest assessment of our spiritual state and a deepening trust in the Messiah are qualities which guarantee our continued spiritual growth.

The heart which is illuminated by the Holy Spirit's application of truth is progressively set free from its bondage to sin and error. "You will know the truth," Jesus said, "and the truth will set you free" (Jn 8:32 NIV). As our hearts, the subconscious root of our personality, are increasingly filled with light, our minds are freed to discover and affirm truth, our wills are freed to obey God, and our emotions are released to feel about all things as God feels about them.

We should note that the immediate goal of illuminated faith is not works or spiritual achievement. Instead, it is *fellowship with God,* leading to fellowship with other believers.

> The error at the root of all false ideas of perfection is this: it is rating our behaviour before God higher than our relation to God—putting conduct before faith, deeds before trust, work before worship. . . . We are not saved by the love we exercise, but by the love we trust. . . . The soul's true and universal perfection is a faith. It is a perfection of attitude rather than of achievement, of relation more than of realization, of truth more than of behaviour. . . . Christian perfection is the perfection not of conduct, character, or creed, but of faith. It is not a matter of our behaviour before God the Judge, but of our relation to God the Saviour.[5]

This fellowship will of course lead to works, to thoughts and words and acts on behalf of the kingdom of God. But these works will emerge primarily out of our fellowship with Christ. And we will be clearly aware that in the deepest sense they are *his* works and not ours—the acts of the risen Christ.

The relationship with God which develops out of repentant faith is particularly focused on Jesus the Messiah. He is the second Adam, the source of all renewed humanity. Whatever renewal takes place in our lives flows from our faith-relationship to him. Instead of inheriting guilt, corruption and death from the first Adam, we now inherit peace, healing and life from the Messiah. "If, because of one man's trespass, death reigned through that one man, much more will those who receive the abundance of grace and the free gift of righteousness reign in life through the one man Jesus Christ" (Rom 5:17).

Because we are united to Jesus the Messiah through faith, we are accepted by God each day as whole and complete. We are received as those who are filled with all his graces, even though our lives may still be shot through with inconsistencies. And we have a new inheritance from the Messiah. Instead of inheriting guilt, bondage to sin, estrangement from God and subjection to the devil, we share in Jesus' victory over human sin and alienation and over the powers of darkness. By faith we can claim *justification* (freedom from guilt because Jesus' righteous acts and sacrificial death have been credited to our account), *sanctification* (freedom from bondage to sin through the inpouring of the life of Christ in our experience, leading to progress in actual holiness), *the Holy Spirit dwelling in our hearts* (so that we have personal fellowship with God), and *authority over the powers of darkness* (the ability to resist and displace demonic agents by calling upon them the judgment Jesus brought upon the devil).

I call these four benefits of redemption *primary elements of renewal* (see figure 2). Building on the preconditions of renewal already dis-

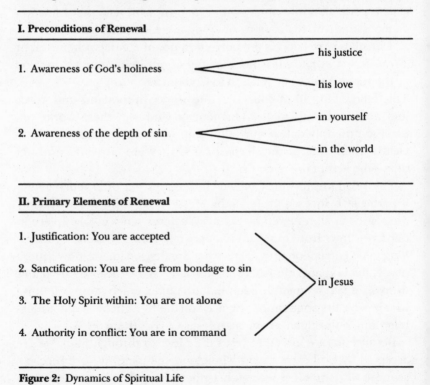

I. Preconditions of Renewal

1. Awareness of God's holiness — his justice
 — his love

2. Awareness of the depth of sin — in yourself
 — in the world

II. Primary Elements of Renewal

1. Justification: You are accepted

2. Sanctification: You are free from bondage to sin

3. The Holy Spirit within: You are not alone

4. Authority in conflict: You are in command

in Jesus

Figure 2: Dynamics of Spiritual Life

cussed—awareness of the holiness of God and of the depth of sin—
they provide the answers needed by the heart wounded by conviction
of sin. Like the three primary colors, they are the source of all the
multicolored splendor of new life in the Messiah. When we shine the
light of the gospel on our analytic prism, the good news divides into
a rainbow with these four elements: justification, sanctification, the
Holy Spirit's indwelling and authority in spiritual conflict. (We can
easily remember these results of the atonement, and the fact that they
are rooted in the Messiah, if we keep in mind the acronym J-S-H-A,
the first letter of each element, which is close to the Jewish way of
writing Jesus, *Yeshua.* See appendix A, figure 3.)

I am uncertain about the value of "Christian mantras," which attempt to build up spirituality by the repetition of phrases like the Jesus
Prayer ("Lord Jesus Christ, have mercy on me, a sinner"). But I do
think we can benefit from deeply fixing in our hearts this fourfold
description of what we inherit through faith in the Messiah. At the
outset of each day, we should hear God saying, *You are accepted,* because the guilt of sin is covered by the righteousness of Christ; *You
are free from bondage to sin* through the power of Jesus in your life; *You
are not alone,* but accompanied by the Counselor, the Spirit of the Messiah; *You are in command,* with the freedom to resist and expel the
powers of darkness.

The four elements of renewal are sometimes presented separately
in Scripture, but they are also often woven together in almost insep-
arable union. Colossians 2 presents three out of the four elements
and relates them to the cross and to union with the Messiah, the
wellspring of spiritual growth: "So then, just as you received Christ
Jesus as Lord, continue to live in him, strengthened in the faith as you
were taught, and overflowing with thankfulness. . . . For in the Messiah all the fullness of the Deity lives in bodily form, and you have
been given fullness in the Messiah, who is the head over every power
and authority" (Col 2:6-10 NIV).

Sanctification, cleansing of our lives from the ruling power of sin,
is no longer symbolized by the limited purging in the Old Covenant
rite of circumcision. It is now death to sin and resurrection to new life
in Christ, symbolized by baptism: "In him you were also circumcised,

in the putting off of the sinful nature, not with a circumcision done by the hands of men but with the circumcision done by the Messiah, having been buried with him in baptism and raised with him through your faith in the power of God, who raised him from the dead. When you were dead in your sins and in the uncircumcision of your sinful nature, God made you alive with Christ" (Col 2:11-13 NIV).

Justification, freedom from the guilt of sin, is accomplished as the Law and the record of our sin are set aside. "He forgave us all our sins, having canceled the written code, with its regulations, that was against us and that stood opposed to us; he took it away, nailing it to the cross" (Col 2:13-14 NIV).

The third of our four elements is mentioned at the end of the text. The basis for our *authority over the powers of darkness* is Jesus' victory over them in the atonement: "And having disarmed the powers and authorities, he made a public spectacle of them, triumphing over them by the cross" (Col 2:15 NIV).

These three elements of spiritual renewal, along with a vital fellowship with the Holy Spirit, are God's free gift to us as we abide in Christ (Jn 15:4). In fact, the measure in which we consciously appropriate these aspects of renewal virtually determines the measure in which we will enjoy spiritual vitality. And so we must look carefully at each of these elements, to make sure we have understood its significance in our own experience.

Optimum spiritual health is in large part a function of spiritual realism. We say persons are psychologically healthy if they have a realistic orientation toward themselves, toward others and toward the world. Realism about ourselves includes an honest assessment of our weaknesses and a confident awareness of our strengths—knowing what we have going against us and what we have going for us. Spiritual health is based on the same kind of realism expanded to include the dimensions of reality known through faith: God's holiness, the depth of our sin, our justification, our sanctification, the indwelling of the Holy Spirit, and our authority over demonic powers. Spiritual realism sheds new light not only on our relationship to God, but also on the way we relate to every other significant person in our lives: family members, peers, authorities and subordinates in our work.

Of course spirituality is more than giving assent to truth. But faith and spiritual honesty establish a *climate of truth* in which God delights to dwell, ennobling our lives by the gifts and power of his Spirit. And the realism of faith is more than assent to distant and abstract propositions. It is a personal trust in Jesus and his redemptive work, and recognition and admission of what is true in our own lives at the most personal level. As we look at each of these ingredients of redemption more closely, we need to evaluate the measure in which our faith is appropriating the fullness of the Messiah.

Justification

The faith which lays claim to justification sets aside the record of our own sin and spiritual achievement and concentrates on "the wholly alien righteousness of Christ," as Luther would say.[6] It looks away from our imperfection—sins committed and righteous deeds left undone—and fixes its attention on the sinless life and saving death of Jesus. Unrecognized sin or pride in works can obscure this view. But the righteousness which makes us "accepted in the beloved" is *his* righteousness, not ours. It is the goodness of the Redeemer, which is imputed or reckoned to our account, even though it may not be fully resident in our lives. It is like being declared innocent by a court although we know ourselves to be in fact guilty. Justification is being treated *as if* we were sinless, even though we are not. A simple way of remembering the meaning of *justified* is the phrase "just-as-if-I'd never sinned."

Common sense tells us that this forgiveness, totally free for us although it cost the Son of God his life, is too good to be true. Our conscience tells us to find something in ourselves to justify us—works, repentance, a "state of grace" or an infusion of the life of Jesus. And it is true that all of these things will be present in the soul which exercises justifying faith. But all are virtually impossible unless the heart's deepest foundation is a grateful acceptance of the free gift of the Messiah's righteousness. Common sense, our misinstructed conscience and our pride must be set aside. They must be replaced with *total reliance on the Messiah* for our acceptance with God.

This is indeed "good news." Initially it does strike us as too good to be true. If it were not clearly taught in Scripture, none of us could persist in believing it. But the core of justification by faith is present even in the Old Testament. David speaks of it in the psalm which may describe his own emergence from a period of inner darkness and self-deception after his adultery with Bathsheba (2 Sam 11).

How blessed is he whose transgression is forgiven,
Whose sin is covered!
How blessed is the man to whom the LORD does not impute
   iniquity,
And in whose spirit there is no deceit!
When I kept silent about my sin, my body wasted away
Through my groaning all day long.
For day and night Thy hand was heavy upon me;
My vitality was drained away as with the fever heat of summer.
I acknowledged my sin to Thee,
And my iniquity I did not hide;
I said, "I will confess my transgressions to the LORD";
And Thou didst forgive the guilt of my sin. (Ps 32:1-5 NASB)

This is a classic description of the purifying of the heart through repentant faith. The text speaks of the nonimputation of sin, rather than the imputation to David of the righteousness of the Messiah. But this is natural in the Old Testament context. The reason David could be forgiven was that the Messiah was going to live a perfect life and atone for his sins. David, like modern Christians, was "accepted in the beloved."

In the New Testament this truth is more fully disclosed in the teaching of Paul, especially in his letter to the Romans. Paul insists that all goodness which does not grow out of faith in the Messiah is no better than sin: "For in the gospel a righteousness from God is revealed, a righteousness that is by faith from first to last, just as it is written: 'The righteous will live by faith' " (Rom 1:17 NIV). After dismissing as fictitious the supposed righteousness of both Gentiles and Jews, pagans and orthodox believers, Paul observes: "No one will be declared righteous in his sight by observing the law; rather, through the law we become conscious of sin. But now a righteousness from God, apart from law, has been made known . . . [which] comes through faith in Jesus the Messiah to all who believe. . . . Where, then, is boasting? It is excluded. . . . For we maintain that a man is justified by faith apart from observing the law" (Rom 3:20-22, 27-28 NIV).

"The righteousness from God" is indeed a strange and marvelous concept. It is a righteousness which is not actually present in our lives, but is credited to us *because we have trusted in the one man who really was righteous.* It is righteousness as if we had the moral integrity of the Messiah, when in fact we always fall short of the perfection needed to satisfy God.

It is hard to convince our conscience and our common sense that this imputed righteousness is really given to those who simply believe. The temptation is strong to look for something in our character or our current behavior which determines whether or not God loves and accepts us. And yet Paul says: " 'Abraham believed God, and it was credited to him as righteousness.' Now when a man works, his wages are not credited to him as a gift, but as an obligation. However, to the man who does not work but trusts God who justifies the wicked, his faith is credited as righteousness. . . . The words 'it was credited to him' were written not for him alone, but also for us, to whom God will credit righteousness—for us who believe in him who raised Jesus our Lord from the dead" (Rom 4:3-5, 23-24).

Although Paul clearly states that Abraham was not justified by works (Rom 4:2), James seems to say the exact opposite:

Do you want evidence that faith without deeds is useless? Was not our ancestor Abraham considered righteous for what he did when he offered his son Isaac on the altar? You see that his faith and his actions were working together, and his faith was made complete by what he did. . . . You see that a person is justified by what he does and not by faith alone. (Jas 2:20-24 NIV)

But clearly James is contrasting an abstract, theoretical belief that does not move the heart with one that is real enough to issue in changed behavior:

What good is it, my brothers, if a man claims to have faith but has no deeds? Can such faith save him? . . . As the body without the spirit is dead, so faith without deeds is dead. (Jas 2:14, 26 NIV)

Abraham's faith led him into a wilderness to sacrifice everything he held dear in order to obey God. And so the faith which justifies is also a faith which inevitably and immediately leads to sanctification, to growth in character and behavior. It is a dynamic and transforming force—"faith active in love," as Luther says.

If justification is always so closely associated with sanctification and deeds, why does Paul put so much stress on faith apart from deeds as the basis of justification? There is a deep psychological and spiritual insight behind this. Although our conscience can be deluded into a kind of superficial confidence that God accepts us on the basis of our character and behavior, in our deepest heart we know that nothing but perfection can satisfy an infinitely perfect God. And we know we are not perfect!

Thus the spirituality of achievement is undercut by deep currents of anxiety. True goodness can only flow forth from a heart which has been cleansed by a total and confident reliance on the free gift of salvation in the Messiah. Such a heart is constantly moved by a grateful awareness of the huge and continually accumulating debt of sin which is canceled as God accepts us in the Messiah. "For Christ's love compels us, because we are convinced that one died for all . . . that those who live should no longer live for themselves but for him who died for them and was raised again" (2 Cor 5:14-15 NIV).

"I am accepted"—accepted as though my life displayed the spiritual perfection of the Messiah himself—ought to be the automatic response of our hearts whenever we wake, like the compass needle that always points north. This is a response which is always relevant to our current spiritual condition. We never make such progress in sanctification that we can depend on it for acceptance. And our continuing record of sin and failure never expands beyond the limits of the love of Christ, who has covered our debts for all time, past, present and future.

The insistence of James that *justifying* faith is also *sanctifying* faith is directed against a dead orthodoxy that relaxes all striving for holiness and lives according to the flesh in a deluded confidence that this is "the righteousness of faith." This kind of religion has been called "cheap grace" by Dietrich Bonhoeffer.[7] It is called "presumption" by spiritual theologians. Persons presuming on God's grace may be backslidden Christians, or they may not be Christians at all. Protestants in the Reformed tradition have held that professing Christians who stay permanently backslidden or who drift away from the church altogether may never have really experienced justifying faith, but have rested in a surface mental assent to doctrine.

Catholics have been characteristically wary of presumption. They have sought to guard against this by teaching that Christians can never rest in the assurance that God has saved them, but must strive to persevere to the end, depending by faith on Christ's saving work.

This seems to put too much weight on human work and initiative to be satisfactory either theologically or psychologically. It grounds acceptance with God on performance rather than unconditional love. This in turn dampens faith and love, because, realistically, we can have little confidence in our ability to perform. Thus our attention becomes focused on our own efforts instead of on God's grace and love.

Most Protestants have therefore held that assurance of salvation is necessary for healthy spirituality. Christians need to know that they have a secure status as adopted sons and daughters of God in order to behave naturally in his presence. For us to be phasing in and out of sonship according to our behavior, constantly testing our experience to make sure we are in a "state of grace," short-circuits the reality of grace.

The Scriptures, however, do insist that assurance is partly conditioned on behavior and experience. Real Christians, those who are vitally engrafted into the "true vine" (Jn 15:1-8), will not fall away from salvation as do those who are not true branches, who have a dead and temporary faith. But they may fall away from *the assurance* that they are real Christians.

The Bible teaches that this assurance is gained in three ways. The first is naked faith in Christ. As Luther insisted, there are times when our experience is so clouded that we can only cling to a bare faith directed away from ourselves, and toward Jesus, as the ground for assurance. At these times we find that all we can do is look outward at Jesus on the cross, just as the Israelites gazed at the bronze serpent on a pole to be healed of their snakebites: "As Moses lifted up the serpent in the wilderness, so must the Son of man be lifted up, that whoever believes in him may have eternal life" (Jn 3:14-15).

But Paul warns us also to "examine yourselves to see whether you are in the faith; test yourselves" (2 Cor 13:5 NIV). John's first letter offers a series of tests to determine whether our belief in the Messiah is really faith active in love: constant efforts to obey God's commands (2:3-5; 3:21-24), love of others (2:9-11; 3:11-18; 4:7-21; 5:1-5), hatred of the world system (2:15-17), faith in sound doctrine (2:24), and efforts to purify our lives from patterns of continuing sin (2:29—3:10) as well as personal faith in Jesus as the Messiah (3:23; 4:15; 5:1, 10-13).

Besides gaining assurance by naked faith and the inspection of our lives, we also have the inner witness of the Holy Spirit. "The Spirit himself testifies with our spirit that we are God's children" (Rom 8:16 NIV). A healthy Christian will be enjoying or striving toward all three modes of assurance of salvation. One who is in stress and difficulty may be forced back to naked faith in Christ. But if this is not eventually reinforced by the other two modes, assurance will be eroded, or even temporarily lost.

Sanctification

And so justifying faith, in order to be credible to our own conscience, must also be sanctifying faith. Our experience must be changed to encompass acts of Christian love and communion with the Holy Spirit to such a degree that we know we are *regenerated*, "born again." Regeneration is the initial state of sanctification. And we must be aware that this process of growth in holiness continues throughout our lives. Nothing can stop it, not even the stubborn remnants of residual sin in our personalities. And therefore every day ought to begin with a response of faith to the second element of renewal, sanctification: "I am free from bondage to sin."

This response is relatively easy to make at times in our lives when we have experienced conscious conversion or victory over a particular pattern of sin. It is more difficult at points when God has made us aware of mountains in our lives which need moving, areas of behavior in which we have been continuing to walk in darkness but which are now painfully illuminated by the Spirit's convicting light.

Growth in sanctification should be a lifelong series of alterations in our lives through such crises of conviction. One of the functions of God's law (biblical moral principles which declare God's will for our behavior) is to measure our lives and locate places where they need changing. "The law" comes to us again and again, not only in the pages of Scripture, but also in the warnings or protests of people close to us who can see our failings, however much they may be in the dark about their own. Parents, teachers, the police and other authorities are all personalized forms of the law.

A husband or wife also functions in this same way, serving God as an agent of our sanctification. He or she can see the patterns of sin which are hidden from our own vision by spiritual darkness, and from the world because it sees only the surface of our lives. Most divorces among Christians probably occur because the parties have not realized that *marriage is a contract to aid in one another's sanctification.* Without this realization, we become experts at what is wrong with one another, without recognizing that the information our spouse is giving us about ourselves is an essential aid to our spiritual growth.

Once a major area of need for change has been located, Christians are required by Scripture to believe that change can occur: "What shall we say then? Are we to continue in sin that grace might increase? May it never be! How shall we who died to sin still live in it? . . . [We know that] our old self was crucified with Him, that our body of sin might be done away with, that we should no longer be slaves to sin. . . . Even so consider yourselves to be dead to sin, but alive to God in Jesus the Messiah" (Rom 6:1-2, 6, 11 NASB).

Note that sanctification, like justification, is primarily a matter of faith. The victory over our sin was won by the Messiah in his death and resurrection. Our old self (the Greek text really says *old man* or *old humanity*) was crucified with him, and we were raised up with Christ in a new supernatural vitality which has power to overcome sin: "For sin shall not be master over you, for you are not under law, but under grace" (Rom 6:14 NASB).

We cannot conquer sin by effort and will power alone, but only by an active faith, depending on the free gift of deliverance through the Messianic atonement. Behavior changed by will power alone, without faith or the operation of the Holy Spirit, simply transmutes sin into another form: moral pride and self-righteousness. And the most serious forms of sin cannot be touched by will power, because they are spiritual states below the surface of our actions.

Nevertheless, action, as well as faith, is required if our faith is to be more than a passive or passing notion. By faith we must actively and lovingly obey God, striving to change our thoughts, words, acts, and even our attitudes and emotions. This activity is represented by various metaphors in Paul's teaching on sanctification. It is putting everything we are and have at God's disposal, rather than continuing to serve the slave master, sin: "Therefore do not let sin reign in your mortal body that you should obey its lusts, and do not go on presenting the members of your body to sin as instruments of unrighteousness; but present yourselves to God as those alive from the dead, and your members as instruments of righteousness to God" (Rom 6:12-13 NASB).

Sanctification is stripping off the characteristics of the old humanity, like filthy clothing, and reclothing ourselves with Christian behavior: "The night is nearly over; the day is almost here. So let us put aside the deeds of darkness and put on the armor of light. Let us behave decently, as in the daytime, not in orgies and drunkenness, not in sexual immorality and debauchery, not in dissension and jealousy. Rather, clothe yourselves with the Lord Jesus Christ, and do not think about how to gratify the desires of the sinful nature" (Rom 13:12-14 NIV).

Finally, sanctification is executing—putting to death—the residual patterns of sin in our lives, which strive to intimidate us even though they have no power to rule over us, because our sinful nature really died with the Messiah on the cross: "Put to death, therefore, whatever belongs to your earthly nature: sexual immorality, impurity, lust, evil desires and greed, which is idolatry. Because of these, the wrath of God is coming. You used to walk in these ways, in the life you once lived. But now you must rid yourselves of all such things as these: anger, rage, malice, slander, and filthy language from your lips. Do not lie to each other, since you have taken off your old self with its practices and have put on the new self, which is being renewed in knowledge in the image of its Creator" (Col 3:5-10 NIV).

The Holy Spirit Within

"If by the Spirit you put to death the misdeeds of the body, you will live" (Rom 8:13 NIV). This text suggests that putting to death the sinful elements of our personality and replacing them with a new and Christ-like humanity is possible only with the help of the Holy Spirit. Changing those parts of our nature that "work wrong" so that they "work right" is a task only the Messiah can accomplish. Only his Spirit can accomplish redemption in our lives. The work of the cross and the power of the Spirit are indomitable. Thus we should face the largest, most persistent mountains of sinful behavior in our lives and boldly assert the response of faith each morning: "I am not alone in the war against sin."

And so our faith, even one active in loving obedience, is not, by itself, a magical cure for sin. Faith taps into the energy of resurrection life in the Messiah. The exercise of faith is like the shifting of gears which enables an automobile engine to move the car forward. But this energy is available only in a relationship with the indwelling Spirit of God. *Victory over sin* without *communion with God* would be a meaningless contradiction, since God's highest will for our lives is communion with him. A legalistically faultless life lived without fellowship with God would be hollow. But a flawed life which struggles to maintain communion with God is still pleasing to him and may be full of vital spirituality.

The *Spirit of God* is also called in Scripture the *Spirit of the Messiah.* When Jesus was about to leave his disciples and return to the Father, he promised, "I will not leave you as orphans; I will come to you" (Jn 14:18 NIV). He would return in the indwelling presence of his Spirit: "I will ask the Father, and he will give you another Counselor to be with you forever—the Spirit of truth" (Jn 14:16-17 NIV). Through the indwelling Spirit, the Father and Son would be in the closest communion with believers: "If anyone loves me, he will obey my teaching. My Father will love him, and we will come to him and make our home with him" (Jn 14:23 NIV).

All believers in Jesus the Messiah are assured in Scripture that the

Spirit of God dwells in them. "Do you not know that your body is a temple of the Holy Spirit, who is in you, whom you have received from God?" (1 Cor 6:19 NIV). "And if anyone does not have the Spirit of the Messiah, he does not belong to the Messiah" (Rom 8:9 NIV). Believers in the Messiah, who are so closely joined to him by his Spirit that they are called members of his body (1 Cor 6:15), can affirm at an even deeper level the conviction of the psalmist:

Where can I go from your Spirit?
Where can I flee from your presence?
If I go up to the heavens, you are there;
    if I make my bed in the depths, you are there.
If I rise on the wings of the dawn,
    if I settle on the far side of the sea,
even there your hand will guide me,
    your right hand will hold me fast.
If I say, "Surely the darkness will hide me
    and the light become night around me,"
even the darkness will not be dark to you. (Ps 139:7-12 NIV)

Christians act as though fellowship with the Holy Spirit were very hard to establish. Actually it is very difficult to avoid! All that is necessary is for the believer to open up to that divine Reality in the center of consciousness which is the most fundamental fact of a Christian's inner life. Christians are "led by the Spirit of God" (Rom 8:14). A husband living under the same roof with a wife would find it difficult to forget her presence, even if she were invisible, because of the many practical signs of her help. We are living just that closely with the Spirit of God, and the marks of his assistance to us every day are just as plain.

There are distinctive services which the Spirit has been sent to perform in our lives. As we give attention to these ministries, our awareness of him will grow. The first of these is perfecting our sanctification. He is called "the Holy Spirit," and he intends to make our lives an environment of holiness for his indwelling. He is especially active in contending against our sin: "Live by the Spirit, and you will not gratify the desires of the sinful nature. For the sinful nature desires what is contrary to the Spirit, and the Spirit what is contrary to the sinful nature. . . . The fruit of the Spirit is love, joy, peace, patience, kindness, goodness, faithfulness, gentleness and self-control" (Gal 5:16-17, 22 NIV). His primary aim is to conform us to Jesus, to make our personalities more and more reflect the grace of the Messiah. As we give increasing attention to making our lives obedient to this concern, he will increasingly manifest himself to us (Jn 14:21).

A second principal ministry of the Spirit is to lead us into the understanding of divine truth, since it is through faith in truth that we grow spiritually. The Holy Spirit is also called "the Spirit of truth" (Jn 14:17; 15:26). "The Counselor, the Holy Spirit, whom the Father will send in my name, will teach you all things and will remind you of everything I have said to you" (Jn 14:26 NIV). "He will bring glory to me by taking from what is mine and making it known to you" (Jn 16:14 NIV). His ministry of teaching is designed not only to make supernatural realities clear to our understanding, but to reveal to us the glory of God and the Messiah: "I keep asking that the God of our Lord Jesus Christ, the glorious Father, may give you the Spirit of wisdom and revelation, so that you may know him better. I pray also that the eyes of your heart may be enlightened in order that you may know the hope to which he has called you, the riches of his glorious inheritance in the saints, and his incomparably great power for us who believe" (Eph 1:17-19 NIV).

In short, the ministry of the Holy Spirit in the church is to *express the life and personality of Jesus the Messiah through the distinctive personalities of individual believers and to bind believers together into a unified organism, his body, which bears corporate witness to his presence in the world.* In our daily experience the Holy Spirit leads (Rom 8:14) and empowers us (Lk 24:49; Acts 1:8) to carry out the acts of the risen Lord, to do greater things now, than Jesus did before his ascension (Jn 14:12).

The Spirit guides us in our prayer, sweeping us up into the current of Jesus' present priestly intercession (Rom 8:26, 34). He also guides our thinking and enables us to have the mind of the Messiah toward all things (1 Cor 2:7-16). He pours the love of God into our hearts, as Jesus loves others through us (Rom 5:5; 1 Cor 13). He inspires us to be his witnesses, directing our words as we speak (Mt 10:19-20). We should be constantly aware that we are not alone, because the one who has been sent to be our Counselor is active in every phase of our daily lives.

The Holy Spirit's control and empowering of our lives are symbolized in Scripture by the concept of "the fullness of the Spirit." Two types of filling which are distinct and yet related are denoted by this phrase. One usage seems to refer to the equipping of believers with spiritual gifts and energy, either for some specific task or some continuing function in the body of Christ, such as teaching or pastoring (Acts 2:4; 4:31; 6:5; 2 Tim 1:6). The other designates the fine-tuned control and energizing of the Spirit in our lives, which increases as we are sanctified (Rom 8:11-13; Jn 15:4). Every Christian should experience both of these dimensions of fullness. Both are needed to carry out the present ministry of the Messiah in building his kingdom. A powerfully gifted person who shows little of the sanctifying grace of the Spirit's control can be impressive but dangerous, like a runaway buzz saw. On the other hand, a saintly Christian endeavoring to do a work for which he or she is not gifted will be a gracious failure.

The contemporary Pentecostal and charismatic movements emphasize that the fullness of the Spirit should be connected with the exercise of the supernatural gifts *(charismata)* mentioned in 1 Corinthians 12—wisdom, knowledge, faith, healing, miracles, prophecy, discernment of spirits, tongues and the interpretation of tongues. There is no doubt that every congregation of Christians should be enriched by the addition of these gifts, along with other charismata mentioned in Scripture (see Rom 12:6-8; 1 Cor 12:28). These gifts must not be quenched. If they are, the Holy Spirit will be grieved. "Do not put out the Spirit's fire; do not treat prophecies with contempt. Test everything. Hold on to the good" (1 Thess 5:19-21 NIV). "Therefore, my brothers, be eager to prophesy, and do not forbid speaking in tongues" (1 Cor 14:39 NIV).

On the other hand, the demand that *every* Christian must manifest one of these gifts to be recognized as Spirit-filled runs against the express teaching of Scripture on the diversity of spiritual gifts.

For just as the body is one and has many members, and all the members of the body, though many, are one body, so it is with the Messiah. . . . If the foot should say, "Because I am not a hand, I do not belong to the body," that would not make it any less a part of the body. . . . The eye cannot say to the hand, "I have no need of you," nor again the head to the feet, "I have no need of you." . . . God has appointed in the church first apostles, second prophets, third teachers, then workers of miracles, then healers, helpers, administrators, speakers in various kinds of tongues. Are all apostles? Are all prophets? Are all teachers? Do all work miracles? Do all possess gifts of healing? Do all speak with tongues? Do all interpret? But earnestly desire the higher gifts. (1 Cor 12:12, 15, 21, 28-31)

Paul means by "the higher gifts" those which are more useful in edifying the rest of the body of Christ (1 Cor 14:1-5). Even above these gifts, he places the exercise of love toward other members of the body (1 Cor 13).

It is interesting how both Pentecostals and non-Pentecostals try to get around the clear implications of this set of texts. The older Pentecostal theology insisted that "the fullness of the Spirit" is equivalent to "the baptism of the Holy Spirit," which is received after conversion and is always accompanied by the gift of tongues. But given Paul's statement that not all believers will speak in tongues, this theology is bound to discourage believers who do not receive this gift. It may force the manufacture of false tongue speaking through autohypnosis. Persons holding this theology are almost programmed to divide the church. This is because they assign first- and second-class ranks to believers who are equally mature and gifted spiritually, but in differing ways.

More recent Pentecostal thought finds that "the baptism of the Spirit" in Scripture seems too closely related to justification and union with Christ to be separated from the believer's initial rebirth. Many charismatics today teach that it is more biblical to think of every Christian as potentially filled with the Spirit. In any case, one experience of infilling is definitely not enough. The Greek in Ephesians 5:18 really says "keep on being filled with the Spirit." Certainly the Christians described in Acts experienced multiple fillings with the Spirit.

The division and uneasiness between Christians who speak in

tongues and those who do not is sad. The clear teaching of Scripture is that both groups need one another. As Jeremy Rifkin has suggested, the two groups should join in promoting spiritual renewal in the church, because they have complementary strengths and weaknesses.[8] In both concepts and structures, Pentecostals are strong on *ardor;* non-Pentecostals on *order.* Pure charismatic movements can become superstitious and disorganized, while pure noncharismatic ministries can become dead and rationalistic. The hope of the future lies in congregations which can admit the full spectrum of gifts described in the New Testament. In such congregations all the gifts can help one another and work together, and no gift will be quenched.

Authority in Spiritual Conflict

Readers may find it difficult to make a meaningful response of faith to the fourth primary element of renewal, authority over the powers of darkness. Most Christians are not aware that they are involved in spiritual warfare. Some may be theoretically committed to the existence of real demonic agents, but few are alert to the operations of fallen angels in everyday life. And yet the Bible makes it plain that if we are vigorously working for God, we will run up against his opponents: "Be sober, be watchful. Your adversary the devil prowls around like a roaring lion, seeking some one to devour" (1 Pet 5:8).

As Christians we not only run up against demonic agents in a defensive way, we also take the offense: "Put on the whole armor of God, that you may be able to stand against the wiles of the devil. For we are not contending against flesh and blood, but against the principalities, against the powers, against the world rulers of this present darkness, against the spiritual hosts of wickedness in the heavenly places" (Eph 6:11-12). We are continuously subject to attack at the devil's initiative. But we are also continually attacking his forces, as we struggle to advance the Messiah's kingdom through the proclamation and demonstration of the gospel.

All this raises another question. How do we become sensitized to spiritual conflict? How do we know when we are up against the devil? The Bible speaks of the *discernment of spirits* as a specific gift given to some Christians. But all believers can develop some ability to detect the operations of the devil.

First, as Paul says, "We are not ignorant of his devices" (2 Cor 2:11 KJV). We know his characteristic modes of operation. In this context, Paul is concerned "lest Satan should get an advantage of us" through resentment between Christians, unhealed by mutual forgiveness. This points up two ways in which the devil normally works: dividing the body of Christ and using unhealed resentment as a gun emplacement for firing accusations (see Eph 4:27).

Chapter five gives us a check list of the other characteristic strategies of darkness. Satan is obviously active in *temptation,* especially in luring us toward snares which would destroy our ability to serve the Messiah. As his names indicate, he is an *accuser* and a *slanderer.* Whenever we find accusation dominating our minds or the minds of others, especially with an apparent admixture of lies, we may be dealing with the devil.

The devil's effort may be to accuse others in our minds, or to accuse us in theirs—or both. He will frequently approach us with his own Satanic caricature of our needs and weaknesses, accusing us in our own minds. In doing this he will pretend to bring the conviction of the Holy Spirit. Or, when the Spirit really is working, the devil may attempt to dull that conviction, giving us counterfeit reassurance. Or he may accuse us at the same time that the Spirit is bringing conviction, turning contrition into despair.

In any case, the inevitable effect of his work as a counterfeit comforter is either insensitivity to sin, or else depression and discouragement. One of the oldest rules in the book for detecting evil spirits is that if our minds are gripped with despair and darkness, then it is not the Holy Spirit working on us; for his conviction of sin is always accompanied by hope for deliverance.

This raises an important point. How can we tell that we are dealing with demonic agents when many of their characteristic strategies employ the temptations, doubts, lies and slanders common to the flesh and the world?

There is a simple response to this question. The powers of darkness do not afflict us aimlessly. There is usually design in their operations, and the design centers on blocking the expansion of the Messianic kingdom. Much of our discernment of Satanic powers comes as we follow the Holy Spirit's guidance in mission and ministry. As we begin initiatives for the kingdom, events will turn in a direction precisely calculated to block our efforts. These events will often be enveloped in a cloud of lies, accusations and misunderstandings, which is the devil's native atmosphere. If all of this comes with an especially disabling power behind it, Satan is probably involved.

Still, there is a need for caution in attributing every bad turn of events to the devil. Even more care is needed in diagnosing individual cases of depression, including our own. Even the Puritans understood that depression could originate in physical needs (lack of sleep, bad nutrition), special psychological factors (a "melancholy temperament"), lack of belief in God's promises, demonic attacks or a combination of these four causes. Today, with an understanding of psychodynamics and the chemical basis of much mental illness, we ought to be ready to consult Christian psychotherapists whenever we encounter depressions which seem outside the framework of kingdom advance and are resistant to counseling and prayer. Lithium carbonate and other medicines may create an emotional foundation for faith, where our counseling would only aggravate an illness.

What response of faith is appropriate in cases where we are fairly sure we have run up against demonic operations? Most modern Christians would despair of ever reaching this certainty, or of doing much about it once reached. But the Scripture gives us much encouragement. Even before his death and resurrection, Jesus gave the disciples "authority to tread upon serpents and scorpions, and over all the power of the enemy" (Lk 10:19). And Paul tells the Roman Christians, "The God of peace will soon crush Satan under your feet" (Rom 16:20 NIV). The power to destroy the works of darkness, which Scripture ascribes to Jesus (Gen 3:15; 1 Jn 3:8), is now ours also, through our union with the Messiah.

Every Christian who exercises this authority is a terror to the powers of darkness. As we follow the Spirit in mission, we are not fighting a defensive war. Jesus promised, "I will build my church; and the gates of hell shall not prevail against it" (Mt 16:18 KJV). Healthy Christians become targets for the enemy, not because they are vulnerable, but because they are treading on the devil's tail!

The Bible does not give us rituals of exorcism or other detailed instructions on how to respond when we run up against demonic agents. It simply says, "Submit yourselves therefore to God. Resist the devil and he will flee from you" (Jas 4:7). As we feel the Spirit leading us to offer this resistance, either in a verbal address or by the whole thrust of our life in faith and mission, we should count on the fact that the devil will have to back off and give ground. Paul did not perform rituals or debate matters with the demons he expelled in Acts 16:18 and 19:12. A mere word of command was enough. The missionary John Nevius found that demons would leave possessed individuals when they were simply surrounded by an atmosphere of prayer, Scripture reading and singing hymns.[9]

We need to remember, however, that demonic agents attack us at every point where we have failed to "put on the whole armor of God" (Eph 6:11), that is, to "put on the Lord Jesus Christ" (Rom 13:14). Thus repelling an assault of Satan may involve counseling that probes for residual patterns of sin, especially unbelief or resentment, which give the devil footholds. It may also involve testing an individual's assurance of justification and relationship to the Holy Spirit.

Actually all the primary elements of spiritual renewal are interactive and interdependent. They are like the intermediate frequency stages on old FM tuners. If any one is disordered, it will disorder the others. In the same way, as we tune up each primary element of renewal—justification, sanctification, relationship to the Spirit, and the exercise of authority in spiritual conflict—each of the others becomes stronger. The same degree of interaction holds also between individual and corporate elements of renewal, and among corporate elements themselves, which we must now move on to examine.

Discussion Questions

Recommended supplemental reading: chapter 4 in *Dynamics*. Scripture for meditation: Romans 4, 6, 8; Ephesians 6:10-20

Section 1: Justification

1. What is *justification*?

2. Why is it vital that we understand that justification and all other spiritual benefits are rooted in *faith*?

3. What is the difference between *imputed righteousness* and *infused righteousness*? Why is this difference important?

4. How well understood do you think justification is in today's church? What effects does this have in the lives of believers?

5. Do you find it hard to avoid belittling sin in your life, on the one hand, and despair about it, on the other?

6. Have you ever been unsure that you were a Christian? What insights has this chapter given you into how you can be sure?

Section 2: Sanctification

1. What is *sanctification*? How does it differ from *justification*?

2. What does *regeneration* mean? How is it related to sanctification?

3. How can moral codes cause us trouble as Christians? In what way are they vital to our spiritual growth?

4. What responsibility do we have to bring one another to account for our characteristic patterns of sin? Why is this especially important in a marriage?

5. What areas of sanctification are easiest to neglect?

Section 3: The Holy Spirit Within

1. How much do you think the average church member knows about the Holy Spirit?

2. How does the Spirit relate to the other two Persons of the Trinity?

3. What distinctive ministries does the Spirit perform in our lives?

4. What does it mean to be "filled with the Spirit"? When and how have you experienced his filling?

5. Why is it important to distinguish between the *gifts* and *graces* of the Spirit?

6. What strengths and weaknesses do you see in charismatic renewal? How can we build on its strengths while avoiding its weaknesses?

Section 4: Authority in Spiritual Conflict

1. Some Christians feel we should "let God take care of the devil" and keep our minds on Jesus. How would you evaluate this approach?

2. Why is it so difficult for us to detect the wiles of the devil? How can

Christian believers get help in discernment?

3. How can we distinguish between the operation of Satan, the flesh, the world and psychological factors? How important is it for us to do this?

4. Is there any set formula for resisting the devil? Can the average Christian do this effectively?

5. What is the connection between our flesh, conformity to the world and the strategies of Satan?

Dynamics of Corporate Renewal

8

If we really believe in Jesus, we know he is the Messiah. We also know that we are joined to him in all his kingly glory. We know he is the second Adam who has brought forth a new humanity, and we know we are part of that new race. We know that he is a perfect priest who has offered a perfect sacrifice, and that God accepts us as perfect because of this. Therefore, our consciences should be void of guilt and our hearts full of gratitude, no matter how poorly we have lived out this freedom. We know that his kingly power can conquer sin and rule in our thoughts, words and actions, and we are committed to this rule. We know that he is very close to us, that he has taken up residence in our lives and wants to be more intimately related to us than any other person. We know that he has broken the powers of darkness and has equipped us to resist and destroy their influence.

As we live in the focused light of this knowledge, we will continually be spiritually renewed. Our object should be to keep the visual field of our minds full of this truth—to walk in the light of truth, as if it were a spotlight accompanying our steps across the stage of daily experience. As the apostle John says, "I have no greater joy than to hear that my children are walking in the truth" (3 Jn 4 NIV).

Of course the surrounding world, the devil and our own residual sin will try to push us out of this circle of light, in one direction or another. Again and again, they will seek to move us away from the light of truth so that our vision of ourselves (both our gifts and our needs) is clouded, or so that our awareness of God (both his holiness and his loving affirmation) is dimmed. One of my teachers used to say that the slightest lie about ourselves or about God, if admitted and believed, can be like a cloud which interrupts the sunshine of God's presence in our hearts.

The Puritans noted that Christians tend to drift out of the light in one of two directions. On the one hand, the devil strives to move us into *presumption,* in which we relax our hold on sanctification and "go native"—walking in the flesh without the Spirit's control and leading. If this fails or we turn to God, the devil tries to move us into *despair,* adopting his estimate of our gifts and relationship with God. Often he first tempts us to walk in the flesh and then holds this up to us in accusation to drive us into despair. This strategy is transparently simple, but maddeningly effective.

Besides twisting our views of ourselves and of God, the dynamics of spiritual death will distort our relationships with others. These relationships are critically important in maintaining spiritual vitality—especially those with our spouse, children and parents, which form the spiritual ecosystem of the family. Also significant are our friends, peers and those who are in authority over us, or to whom we are authority figures. We must be especially careful to walk in the light in these relationships and to have our thinking about them thoroughly illuminated by the Holy Spirit and the Word of God.

Beyond these relationships, of course, is a whole world of people who need the freeing reign of Christ in their lives. The Messiah is *in mission* toward these people, as well as to those closer to us. And he wants us to be agents of his saving purpose toward them. *We cannot really stay close to him without following him in this outward movement of mission.*

In the same way, however, we cannot stay close to him in fellowship without talking with him about our feelings toward others. We need to sense his concerns for those close to us and for those who are more distant. And we cannot serve or help others except as we depend on Jesus in prayer for the answers to their spiritual needs and the solutions to their problems. *Prayerful dependence on the risen Lord is essential to our advancing his rule.*

But there is another way that we relate to those close to us who are Christians: we draw strength from their spiritual gifts and give strength to them through ours. God has drawn us together like living stones to form a house in which he delights to dwell—the ultimate dwellingplace for which tents and buildings have been poor substitutes (1 Pet 2:5). But this temple is also the body of Christ, a living organism moved and controlled by his Spirit. We cannot be strong in the Messiah without being enriched by the other members of his body and, in turn, enriching them. Abiding in Christ means staying in touch with other parts of his body (Jn 15:7). *Being in community with members of the body of Christ* is essential to spiritual renewal.

Finally, to stay close to Jesus we have to know his heart and mind. In our minds, the control room and engine house of our lives, we must know Jesus' outlook. Our thinking about the persons and things that are closest to us must be illuminated by the Holy Spirit. Our whole life-and-world view must be theologically integrated, so that we think biblically. *We cannot stay close to Jesus without having his outlook on everything.*

These four corporate dimensions of life in the Messiah must be added to the diagram which lists preconditions and primary elements of renewal (see figure 3). They are four essential ways in which we must "abide in Christ" if we are to be fully renewed by his Spirit. They are so important in the development of spiritual renewal that we can call them *secondary elements of renewal.* As secondary colors are derived from primary colors, these secondary elements of renewal draw out the larger, corporate implications of the primary elements. Primary responses of faith are centered in individual Christians, as they ap-

I. Preconditions of Renewal

1. Awareness of God's holiness — his justice / his love

2. Awareness of the depth of sin — in yourself / in the world

II. Primary Elements of Renewal

1. Justification: You are accepted

2. Sanctification: You are free from bondage to sin

3. The Holy Spirit within: You are not alone

4. Authority in conflict: You are in command

in Jesus

III. Secondary Elements of Renewal

1. Mission: following Jesus into the world, presenting his gospel — in proclamation / in social demonstration

2. Prayer: depending on the power of the risen Christ — individually / corporately

3. Community: uniting with the body of Christ — in microcommunities / in macrocommunities

4. Theological integration: having the mind of Christ — toward revealed truth / toward your culture

Figure 3: Dynamics of Spiritual Life

propriate the fruits of his redemptive work. Secondary responses of faith move beyond individual growth to encompass the world, the church and the whole of life and thought. (See appendix A, figure 4.)

Mission

The secondary dimensions of renewal are all drawn from the early church's experience of new life in the Messiah, as described in Luke's Acts of the Apostles (which might better be called the Acts of the Risen Lord). All these dimensions are vitally related to the expansion of the Messianic kingdom, spreading like leaven through the pagan society of the Roman Empire.

At the beginning of Acts, the apostles ask the risen Messiah, "Lord, are you at this time going to restore the kingdom to Israel?" (Acts 1:6 NIV). Still gripped by the common vision of immediate peace and prosperity through the Messiah's reign, they are unconsciously trying to evade the long period of spiritual warfare needed to spread the kingdom, to gather the elect from all ages of world history, and to allow the followers of Jesus to become like him through sharing the way of the cross.

Jesus in turn evades their question. "It is not for you to know the times or dates the Father has set by his own authority. But you will receive power when the Holy Spirit comes on you; and you will be my witnesses in Jerusalem, and in all Judea and Samaria, and to the ends of the earth" (Acts 1:7-8 NIV). The apostles were revealing the natural gravitation of their hearts away from outward mission and toward self-centered enjoyment of kingdom blessings. Jesus responds by telling them that the greatest blessing they can know within ordinary history—the full empowering of the Holy Spirit—will only come to them in the context of outward movement in mission.

If we want to "abide in the Messiah," we must go where he wants to go. The New Testament makes it clear that in order to stay with him we must join the great victory march through history, which is the Christian mission: "But thanks be to God, who always leads us in triumphal procession in Christ and through us spreads everywhere the fragrance of the knowledge of him" (2 Cor 2:14 NIV). God has given us the dangerous vocation of being catalysts either for conversion or for the rejection of the gospel: "For we are to God the aroma of Christ among those who are being saved and those who are perishing. To the one we are the smell of death; to the other, the fragrance of life" (2 Cor 2:15-16 NIV).

God has permitted differing styles and models of this evangelistic mission to exist. Some American evangelicals have developed a vigorous, pushy, hard-sell approach to the gospel which wins many and turns off others. The latter may be reached by the quieter witness of Christians who live their faith with integrity and wait for the Spirit to move their neighbors to ask the reason for their hope (1 Pet 3:15). But no Christian who wants to be spiritually renewed can be indifferent to the spiritual fate of others.

The apostles do not harangue believers to "witness," as do some modern pastors intent on church growth. They assume that in a church filled with the Spirit, God himself will be engineering the occasions for witness and that these will unfold with the naturalness of the dialog in a good play. Moreover, they assume that all Christians will "be wise in the way you act toward outsiders" and "make the most of every opportunity" (Col 4:5 NIV).

This means that every Christian must consciously be in a witnessing stance toward all persons who are not already members of the Messianic kingdom. First of all, we should be filled with redemptive concern for family members, friends and everyone at work: superiors, subordinates and peers. The application sections of Paul's letters repeatedly insist that all these relationships should be conducted with Christian love, respect, forbearance, obedience and forgiveness. Christian mission demands that wherever we find hostility, resentment or any other kind of static disturbing our communication with others, we must resolve it so that we may be clear witnesses to the gospel. All too often we become apathetic and use one another as impersonal instruments. But the spiritual situation demands that we be concerned for the welfare of everyone around us, not overlooking their eternal destiny.

Actually all human beings witness to one another, whether or not they choose to do so. Those who are "children of disobedience," following "the course of this world" (Eph 2:2), project the world's magnetic field. Unless we are walking in light, they will draw us into patterns of life that do not have God's kingdom at the center. If we are walking in the Spirit, on the other hand, we will be consciously or unconsciously drawing them toward the magnetic field of the Messianic kingdom. Either they will win us to the world, for a season, or we will win them to Christ or else arouse in them an increasing resistance to his will. But our relationship to others is never religiously neutral. People are always moving toward or away from God; and we are always either walking in light reaching out to others, or joining them as they walk in darkness. "He who is not with me is against me," says Jesus (Mt 12:30); but also, "He that is not against us is for us" (Mk 9:40).

But what about those with whom we do not have direct contact? Actually the media of the Information Age bring us constantly in touch with the spiritual and material needs of persons and groups throughout the world. Our exposure to their problems can create depression or apathy, if we respond in darkness. But it can also create positive concern and prayer, if we are responding in the Spirit and in light.

In the great missionary explosion of the Second Evangelical Awakening, *information* and *prayer* were the catalysts for action. The same can be true today. A very effective means for raising our awareness of unreached people groups is the Frontier Missions' prayer booklet from Ralph Winter's Center for World Missions.[1] This guide for family devotions shares information each day about one of the 16,750 people groups on our planet who have no indigenous Christian church and no culturally close witness to the gospel. Winter has developed a plan for mission funding which involves saving pocket change at each evening devotional period, a Western equivalent of one tribe's practice of saving rice at each meal to pay for outreach to a neighboring tribe. This "loose change fellowship" is generating new sources of income which may reinvigorate frontier evangelism among mainline denominations.

Winter's work has made American Christians aware that they enjoy a disproportionate share of *everything*—not only of the world's energy and manufactured goods, but also of exposure to the gospel. As we might expect, the huge majority of committed and nominal Christians are in North America, Europe and other parts of the world colonized by Europe. These areas also have "unreached peoples" who are culturally distant from the Christians surrounding them. But the majority of unreached people are in the Muslim world or in areas, like Asia, dominated by older living religions.

The aim of Protestant world missions during the last three centuries has been to expand Christian witness until all the earth should be full of the knowledge of the Messiah, "as the waters cover the sea." But the vast majority of the world's population is not only non-Christian, over 2.3 billion people have never even had the opportunity to hear the gospel. Three centuries of expanding missions, and the earth is still a sea of ignorance!

Yet most evangelistic and missionary effort is still devoted to reaching and awakening nominal Christians. The majority of these forces are concentrated in the "settled" areas where Christian witness already exists. The massive concentration of wealth and Christian talent in America could be providential. But in both the financial and spiritual realms, Americans tend to think in terms of a closed system which ignores the needs outside America. This reveals a tremendous spiritual vitamin deficiency: a lack of the vital renewal ingredient of mission concern. We have the same tendency that the apostles had: we want to settle down and enjoy the kingdom *now* instead of expanding it throughout the world. The American dream of dynasty building and material prosperity is operating where the vision of the Messianic kingdom ought to be!

Some measure of American prosperity, both material and spiritual, may indeed be in God's plan. But our self-centered pursuits are dangerous to our physical and spiritual health! While Americans concentrate on the hard problem of finding a diet that a lack of will power cannot sabotage, the rest of the world is grappling with crushing poverty and famine, and resenting our corporate indifference toward it. Parts of the underdeveloped world are in spiritual darkness also, but our uncaring prosperity makes it unlikely that Third World nations will expect light from American sources. Meanwhile, the American church may be dying spiritually, because it is unconcerned with the material needs of others and because it is hoarding spiritual resources which could bring the rest of the world to the Messiah!

The American laity may be the sleeping giant that holds the key to effective world mission. Richard Hutcheson has shown that every past spiritual awakening has been an age of lay activism. In these eras, the clergy have been relegated to the roles of coach and cheering section while the laity played the game. During the great evangelical awakenings, laypeople dedicated themselves to the Messianic kingdom with unreserved generosity. They gave their wealth, their time and their energy to the task of extending the rule of Christ both through evangelism and through the reshaping of society.[2]

Today, many countries have closed their doors to full-time missionaries but are still open to "tentmakers"—Christians with knowledge or technical skills to contribute to economic development, who are also motivated to serve as evangelistic agents of Christ the King. J. Christy Wilson has described this avenue of missions in his book *Today's Tentmakers*.[3] Increasing numbers of American laypersons are disengaging themselves from the American dream and following the kingdom vision overseas. Younger Christians who are not yet anchored to a home and family are spending years of internship in the work force overseas, sharing the gospel as they do so. Older Christians are taking early retirement and sacrificing time and comfort to share their expertise abroad. The gratitude of those who are being served by these tentmakers is surely opening hearts to the gospel.

American Christianity would have had a profoundly deepened missionary impact if its laity had, from the very beginning, regarded themselves as tentmaking missionaries. Instead, as we have seen, most laypersons sought to be dynastic leaders. Their primary goals were gaining financial security and social position. They wanted to be pious enough to be prosperous. But the church was not the hub of their lives; it was a spoke on the edge of their concerns. It was not the mission station out of which their kingdom vocation was discerned and supported, but a therapy center supporting their "careers." *Careers* are what result when the Protestant doctrine of vocation is secularized, when the work of the laity is understood as a calling not from God, but from the American society which trains us to be patriotic consumer-producers.

The unconscious concept of both ministers and laypeople is that for the clergy, mission is indeed "full-time Christian work." For laypersons, however, it is a sort of part-time avocation limited to giving a percentage of income to support "real missionaries"—usually somewhere else—while we on the home front limit our mission to verbal witnessing to acquaintances and coworkers. The desire of laypersons to conduct mission on this basis and the willingness of clergy to put up with being a support system for the American dream have crippled our ability to do mission at home and abroad. It has allowed American business to assume a thoroughly secular shape, even while a huge proportion of its work force is made up of professing Christians.

At best, we try to avoid conforming to the ethical corruption of business life and occasionally seek to win individuals to Christ. It never occurs to most of us to pray, "thy kingdom come, on earth as it is in heaven," with the specific shape of our workplace in mind. Few Christians ever pray that their business will stop taking ethical shortcuts and that it will have a constructive impact on the environment, on consumers, on fellow workers and on management, as well as earning a profit for stockholders. They accept the conventional wisdom that "nice guys finish last" and the social Darwinist teaching of "the survival of the fittest." (We are now told by biologists that Darwin did not find this system among the animals, but projected it on nature from his observation of human behavior in the Industrial Revolution.[4]) All this has intimidated us so that we do not recognize that the way American business runs is often not even according to enlightened self-interest.

Our union with the Messiah and his desire to continue his earthly ministry by living his life through us are so strong that we may be said to share his three offices of leadership. We are *priests* as we pray for those near us and draw them into the sphere of God's mercy and blessing. We are *prophets* as we hold a biblical straightedge against whatever is crooked around us. And we are *kings* as we use whatever powers we have to straighten what is crooked, reshaping whatever falls within the scope of our responsibility until it reflects the order of heaven.

All of this has implications for the second aspect of mission, *the social demonstration of the gospel* (figure 3). As Alvin Toffler has commented, businesses are now beginning to recognize that part of their product has to be social progress.[5] Already many of the most successful corporations are working to create jobs and improve living conditions for minorities in adjacent cities. Much of the *structural evil* in American society—the crooked houses we have built by our inattention to kingdom values—can be corrected by a combination of local government and local business initiatives.

But what about structural evil in the rest of the world, especially in the developing countries? Most of the Third World today is involved with one or the other of the two great empires we call the First and Second Worlds. Since the "free world" in the West is so closely associated with Christian values, the very honor of Jesus the Messiah is upheld or impugned by the way Christians are using their freedom. Are they working to transform the institutions of the First World and make its business and government policies subservient to the interests of the Messianic kingdom? We might think that this goal is impossibly idealistic—as Reinhold Niebuhr and others have told us[6]—except for the fact that some measure of this has already occurred in history. As we have noted, during the Second Evangelical Awakening in England, the British Empire was profoundly influenced by kingdom values.

Spiritual liberation accompanied by social/economic/political liberation was the fundamental motif of the Second Awakening. This combination of biblical themes is well suited to today's world problems. Evangelistic outreach is crucial to social liberation. Third World peoples will receive their daily bread and social deliverance as they call on the name of Jesus, for "everyone who calls on the name of the Lord will be delivered" (Rom 10:13). On the other hand, the very credibility of evangelistic missions, and the continued presence of open doors to do it, may depend on the relation between Western multinational corporations and the countries in which they are working.

One of the most realistic and constructive models of this kind of synergism between the Messianic kingdom and business enterprise has been developed by Campus Crusade's Christian Embassy in Washington, D.C. Endeavoring to witness to Third World diplomats, Embassy staff have discovered that they must respond to the tremendous needs for development voiced by these leaders in order to keep their witness credible. What they have done is to go to Christian leaders in corporations working in these nations and present the needs.

This has often led to change and progress. Corporations which have been working against their own interests by ignoring the social injustice in client countries and cooperating with oppressive systems are now promoting development and social reform. This kind of activity may hold the best hope we have of solving the critically interrelated problems of poverty, freedom and world peace. Another group based in Washington which can help inform you about biblical strategies of social transformation is Evangelicals for Social Action, led by theological activists like Ron Sider and futurologist Tom Sine.[7]

Prayer

Jesus had told the apostles: "The Messiah will suffer and rise from the dead on the third day, and repentance and forgiveness of sins will be preached in his name to all nations, beginning at Jerusalem. You are witnesses of these things. I am going to send you what my Father has promised; but stay in the city until you have been clothed with power from on high" (Lk 24:46-49 NIV).

Facing the formidable and largely unexpected task of evangelizing the whole world for the Messiah, the early church went to prayer, waiting for Jesus to pour out his Spirit to empower them for this task (Acts 1:13-14). Only the very presence of the risen Lord could equip them to move outward in mission. And this movement could only be maintained through a continual dependence on him, receiving divine direction and encouragement in prayer.

The outpouring of the Spirit in Acts 2:1-4 permanently equipped the church for mission. Nevertheless, a vigorous missionary movement can only be maintained and expressed by unceasing prayer in the face of obstacles and persecution (1 Thess 5:17). Throughout Acts new occasions of prayer arise out of difficulties, and from these, new ventures of mission are born. The persecutor Saul is converted in answer to the prayers of the dying martyr Stephen (Acts 7:59—8:1). God calls Paul and Barnabas to go on the first mission to the Gentiles out of a prayer meeting in Antioch (Acts 13:1-3).

Because the inward renewing of the church and its outward extension in mission involve spiritual warfare—the displacement of the flesh, the world and the devil—there is a kind of "prayer cycle" involved in building the Messianic kingdom. The cycle begins with *prayer* in the face of extreme difficulty or Satanic counterattack (Acts 1:13; compare 4:24). As God answers by pouring out his Spirit, the church receives *power* for life and witness (Acts 2:1-4; 4:31). The church then *prospers* in its spiritual growth and outward extension (Acts 2:14-47; 4:32-35). This expansion of the kingdom arouses Satanic counterattack in the form of *persecution,* resistance expressed through the world and the flesh. At this point, the cycle must begin again with prayer; for if we halt in discouragement, the growth and outreach of the body of Christ will be stifled.

For these reasons, prayer is one of the most crucial ingredients both in individual spiritual growth and in the renewal and extension of the church. In Exodus the groaning prayers of God's people arouse pity in God's heart, and he sends the deliverer Moses (Ex 2:23-24). Throughout Judges, we find another kind of repeated cycle in which prayer always leads to the raising up of a leader like Moses. The people of God gradually fall away from God-centered, kingdom-centered living as new generations arise. As their hearts are emptied of the divine presence, they begin to suck in the corruptions of the surrounding world, like a squeezed sponge thrown in a puddle. At this juncture God removes his blessing from them, and they begin to experience hardship and defeat. Then, as they groan in their hearts under these punishments, God is again moved to pity and raises up a new deliverer who can bring peace and the rule of God for one generation.

When individual Christians or the church are *passive* about the kingdom of God, they endure this five-part cycle of decline and renewal. This was the characteristic way of life under the Old Covenant. When they become *active* in advancing the kingdom, in the New Testament pattern, the four-part cycle of growth and counterattack in Acts is the norm. In either case, the course of individual and corporate spirituality does not run smoothly, but ebbs and flows. *This is because we are in a spiritual war,* fighting to liberate a planet occupied by the powers of darkness. The characteristic pattern of such a war is advance and retreat under counterattack, in a series of pulsations moving outward until the earth is "filled with the knowledge of the glory of the LORD, as the waters cover the sea" (Hab 2:14).

In the midst of this kingdom warfare, prayer is the most natural expression of our dependence on the Messianic Victor. He has won the ultimate battle. He alone can supply us with the resources to complete the task of spiritual liberation. In prayer we also gain the greatest insights into Jesus' strategy for kingdom warfare. Once I visited a famous harpist's storeroom, in which she kept almost a dozen harps of various sizes. As I plucked the largest, every harp in the storeroom resounded with the same note. In the same way, as believers are swept into the great tide of Jesus' intercession, the Spirit guides each of us into a better understanding of the mind of Christ. Suddenly we begin to harmonize in our plans and concerns, both with him and with one another (Rom 8:26-27, 34).

Therefore prayer is always critically important in the great movements of spiritual awakening. New initiatives in church renewal, evangelistic outreach, the reformation of manners and social reform emerge from prayer meetings. These are sustained and directed by strategic responses which develop out of prayer, just as military tactics evolve out of communication between front-line troops and the home base. The flesh, the world and the devil cannot be dislodged from individual hearts or social structures without the supernatural power of Jesus' resurrection applied by the Holy Spirit. And this comes most frequently in answer to prayer.

Thus the early church won the Roman Empire by the strength of its prayers, even though its theology was often weak and its morale was shaken by repeated waves of persecution. Pedestrians in Roman streets sometimes felt the walls shake from the "Amens!" of Christians in catacombs or hidden rooms. And eventually the walls of the empire collapsed like those of Jericho. The Reformation was preceded by prayer movements combining spirituality with education, as in the schools of the *Devotio Moderna,* which trained Christian humanists who later became Reformers.

Before the Great Awakening, Cotton Mather organized meetings to pray for a new Pentecost to refresh and empower the lagging Puritan movement. He spent 490 days and nights interceding for worldwide spiritual awakening. When the awakening began in 1727, it started in Count Zinzendorf's community, where a round-the-clock prayer meeting for church renewal and global outreach was maintained for one hundred years. The very name of the community, *Herrnhut*, meant "the Lord's watch" and was drawn from the prayer pattern of Isaiah 62:6-7: "I have posted watchmen on your walls, O Jerusalem; they will never be silent day or night. You who call on the LORD, give yourselves no rest, and give him no rest till he establishes Jerusalem and makes her the praise of the earth" (NIV).

To continue and expand the awakening, Jonathan Edwards and others called for quarterly "concerts of prayer." By the nineteenth century these had escalated to midweek prayer meetings devoted to spiritual awakening and missionary outreach. In the Third Evangelical Awakening, which began in 1858, laypeople began to meet *daily* at noontime to express their concerns in prayer. This pattern continued for decades. In the late nineteenth and early twentieth centuries, fundamentalist and Pentecostal movements with grave theological weaknesses and imbalances continued to prosper, however imperfectly, because they continued to pray.

In the late twentieth century, the race is not being won by the brilliant and well organized. Pentecostals have become a "third force" in world Christianity, not because their doctrine is perfect, but because they have given themselves to the praise of God and to intercessory prayer. If we are to be delivered from attempting only what is predictably achievable, we must return to a proper regard for prayer. To quote the great missionary leader William Carey, we must "expect great things of God, and attempt great things for God."

An increase in the *volume* of prayer may not be as important as refinement in the *agenda*. God, as Jesus tells us, is not impressed by the multitude of our words (Mt 6:7-8). He does respond, however, when we ask those things which are closely related to the interests of the kingdom of his Son. God is looking not for perfect Christians, but for those who are deeply attentive to holy purposes. "This is the one

I esteem: he who is humble and contrite in spirit, and trembles at my word" (Is 66:2 NIV). This means that intercession is effective insofar as it is focused in the unfolding of the Messianic kingdom. Kingdom-centered prayer is always heard by God—not only because it is offered in the name of his Son, but because it is accurately aimed at advancing his rule.

Intercessory prayers have become ceremonial vestiges in our churches—rituals which baptize meetings as they begin and bury them when they end. Such prayers ignore the whole panorama of God's work in the world and focus on stifling particularities. How many pastoral prayers have you heard which embraced the scope of God's work throughout the planet, probed the concerns of his kingdom in the whole nation, and dealt adequately with local concerns beyond the needs of your own congregation? Many worship services are monuments to the spiritual self-centeredness of local churches. It is a wonder that many pastoral prayers ever rise higher than the ceiling, when they so rarely embrace anything beyond the walls.

The evangelical movement has become so specialized in its understanding of renewal and mission that its prayers are oriented not toward the kingdom but toward *projects*. J. Edwin Orr comments that God will give us exactly what we request. If we ask him to heal a relative, in one way or another he will do that. If we ask him to help us meet our Sunday-school budget, he will do that. If we ask him to empower an evangelistic crusade, he will do that. And if we ask him to give us a general spiritual awakening, then he will do exactly that.

The current *shape* of the kingdom of Christ cannot be mapped precisely apart from a continual prayer watch, which sweeps out like a radar beam surveying the territory around us. As that beam revolves, it lights up areas where we sense God's concern to bring heaven's order on earth. It also illuminates mountains of Satanic opposition which must be moved if the Messianic rule is to prevail.

Some years ago my wife and I began to pray together with the deliberate aim of developing intercession which was kingdom-centered rather than self-centered. We pictured our whole field of concern as a target made up of concentric circles, ranging outward from ourselves, with the widest interests of the kingdom at the perimeter.

Regularly we start our intercession at the rim and sweep inward, turning up areas of special need and spiritual warfare in world mission, international events, denominations, our nation, our community and our local church. We find that starting with kingdom concerns infuses our own situation with light and meaning. Occasionally, however, we reverse the process, moving outward from the center, to make sure we are not ignoring our own spiritual needs. As we have prayed for Satanic roadblocks to be removed in mainline churches, in our country and throughout the world, we have often found ourselves drawn into the center of what we have been praying for, in spiritual conflict for the prevailing of God's order.

If your concerns are ordered in the perspective of the kingdom, do you have a sense of peace about them, or are you worrying? Anxiety is often a red light on the mind's dashboard that tells us we are not expressing our needs to God and trusting his providence. "Do not be anxious about anything," Paul says, "but in everything, by prayer and petition, with thanksgiving, present your requests to God. And the peace of God, which transcends all understanding, will guard your hearts and your minds in Christ Jesus" (Phil 4:6-7 NIV).

Prayer partners can be an immense help or even a necessity. If you are married, and your spouse shares your faith, regular prayer together is an urgent necessity. Without it, your spiritual achievements may be crippled, and your marriage itself imperiled. With regular prayer, on the other hand, everything we do will have God's hand on it, carrying it through to completion. He delights in our approaching him together. His Son has promised, "If two of you on earth agree about anything you ask for, it will be done for you by my Father in heaven" (Mt 18:19 NIV).

A step beyond this is corporate prayer in prayer groups, which many find is helpful for pastoral support. For many years now we have had such a group meeting in our house regularly. Many significant projects and initiatives have emerged from this prayer time. We have found that for this kind of prayer to remain alive, it must both touch upon the deepest perceived needs of the group and reach out toward a vision of the kingdom.

Often in such groups it helps to perform this simple exercise. Take the main section of the daily paper and tear it into single pages. Give each person a page and ask him or her to read it looking to the Holy Spirit to light up prayer concerns in the news of the world. Then hold these before the Lord in prayer. A little experience with this technique will show you how often we ignore God's power to change world events and meet deep human needs, both spiritual and social.

Much of the time our minds our numbed and unresponsive to spiritual reality as we read and hear the news. We generally restrict our faith entirely to the private areas of our personal lives. Our failure to use the channel of prayer to change history may be the main reason the church has had so little impact in the West in this century. We may be running at five per cent of our potential efficiency in the church, because we are like billionaires who have somehow been persuaded to think they are paupers and have put away the check-books that put at their disposal tremendous economic power.

In church committees prayer is often a minor obligation, but seldom a matter of desperate resort. Our meetings need to be laminated with prayer, not simply introduced and dissolved with a few appropriate words, like civil occasions when the minister is asked to "say a little prayer." The strongest Christian works I know are those which constantly interrupt committee meetings for prayer, turning to God whenever their own wisdom and vision have run out in the course of discussion.

Finally, at the congregational level, and even beyond it in ecumenical meetings, we need to uphold all the work of the church in prayer. In the Western world, our *talking about* God and *working at projects* for him are way out of balance with our *talking to* and *listening to* him. The balance of prayer may be far better in Korea, Africa and other Third World areas where human beings are less impressed with their ability to solve every problem by thought and effort. For more insights and incentives concerning prayer, read David Bryant's helpful books *In the Gap* and *With Concerts of Prayer.*[8]

Community
Western society is almost painfully self-conscious and individualistic compared to other cultures. We approach everything in life, from

economics to salvation, as if each person were a closed monad, an isolated atomic unit. Our competitive work ethos, based on the fearful pattern of "survival of the fittest," may be part of the reason. The pre-Reformation anxiety which made "saving my soul" an exhausting project and the Puritan concern for proving one's election may also have helped to give us this egocentric bias.

To be sure, each person on earth must individually turn from sin and receive Jesus as Lord if he or she is to be part of the new humanity. Repentance and faith are unavoidably individual matters. Forms of Christianity which ignore personal evangelism to concentrate on restructuring society are really living and preaching a gospel different from the one in Scripture.

Still, as Paul says, "None of us lives to himself alone" (Rom 14:7 NIV). Individual believers are not simply isolated "temples of the Holy Spirit." They are "living stones" (1 Pet 2:5) set upon "Jesus the Messiah himself as the chief cornerstone," and they "are being built together to become a dwelling in which God lives by his Spirit" (Eph 2:20, 22 NIV). God not only gathers individual believers to himself, he also commits himself to work among their children and their most distant descendants. The temple he is building is vastly beyond our normal conception of the church. For he is quarrying stones among every generation, in every century, to build what can only be completed in the eternal state.

The image of God's people as the house in which he longs to live shows something of the collective nature of salvation in Scripture. But stones are often identical in size and shape, and they do not give and receive help among one another. Thus Paul has to move from architecture to biology to do justice to the vital interconnection between individual Christians. His master image for the church is the human body. This is an inspired metaphor for the way Christians combine to form a whole which is greater than the sum of its parts, in which the special gifts of each are essential to the others. "The body is a unit, though it is made up of many parts. . . . The eye cannot say to the hand, 'I don't need you!' . . . If one part suffers, every part suffers with it" (1 Cor 12:12, 21, 26 NIV). "Speaking the truth in love, we will in all things grow up into him who is the Head, that is, the

Messiah. From him the whole body, joined and held together by every supporting ligament, grows and builds itself up in love, as each part does its work" (Eph 4:15-16 NIV).

As we have noted, the Protestant Reformers did not clearly point to the kingdom of Christ as a goal to be pursued beyond the concern for individual salvation. This opened the way for self-centeredness to reassert itself after the event of conversion. The Reformation corrected the Catholic understanding of individual salvation, but did not go beyond it to define adequately the collective Christian enterprise. In the same way, the Reformers did not thoroughly grasp the other great collective image of the church, the body of the Messiah. Their treatment of spiritual nurture and growth is still only a corrected individualism, which defines "the means of grace" simply as "the Word of God, the sacraments and prayer."

These elements are vital dynamics of spiritual life. But they are not the whole story. Taken by themselves, they convey an image of lonely spiritual individualism which generations of Protestants continue to live out. Puritan Christians, for example, were like spiritual deep-sea divers, each with his or her own air line up to God through "the means of grace." Each one intent on private spiritual goals viewed others only dimly through clouded faceplates.

This happened because the Reformers did not grasp an important truth. *Among the most vital means of grace are other Christians.* Neither the Bible nor the sacraments will leave the shelf or the sanctuary to rescue a Christian who is too discouraged or backslidden to pray or worship. But a concerned brother or sister will do this again and again! For this reason, Acts indicates that *living in community* is still another way of continuing to "abide in Christ":

> They devoted themselves to the apostles' teaching and to the fellowship, to the breaking of bread and to prayer. . . . All the believers were together and had everything in common. Selling their possessions and goods, they gave to anyone as he had need. Every day they continued to meet together in the temple courts. They broke bread in their homes and ate together with glad and sincere hearts, praising God and enjoying the favor of all the people. And the Lord added to their number daily. (Acts 2:42-47 NIV)

Evidently there is something so spiritually healthy about this level of community that it is irresistibly attractive to outsiders—or, as the text suggests, it provides a culture so nurturing that God can safely add new converts every day.

If you have spent much time within a Christian community or in a good summer conference ministry, you know that *the spiritual atmosphere of the group* supplies a lift to individuals that you cannot work up on your own and which is seldom duplicated in ordinary church life. The American dream dismantles the body of Christ into component family units pursuing dynastic success. Christians under these conditions draw spiritual strength not from one another, as the Scriptures prescribe, but from one or two church meetings a week in which there is little interaction. Sunday worship is a sacred ritual with audience participation or a sacred classroom with added announcements. These brief gatherings do indeed convey grace. But they are pale compared to the New Testament example: "When you come together, everyone has a hymn, or a word of instruction, a revelation, a tongue or an interpretation. All of these must be done for the strengthening of the church" (1 Cor 14:26 NIV).

We know from history and current experience that it *is* possible to fire up a local congregation so that it becomes a spiritual atomic pile, creating a reaction whose energy goes far beyond the church walls. But just as we must move outward consciously in mission and prayer, so we must make a deliberate effort to move outward in sharing our gifts with the rest of the local body and receiving help from others.

For this reason, each local congregation must seek the full release and development of spiritual gifts in every member. This is done primarily through instructing every member in the dynamics of spiritual growth and by giving prayer its proper priority at every level of congregational life. The church's task is to locate and call forth the spiritual gifts of each church member, so that every individual is aware of the grace and strength she or he has to give to others. If prayer and ministry are focused on equipping the laity for ministry, God will surely bless each member and the whole church, for Jesus has promised, "Ask and it will be given to you; seek and you will find; knock and the door will be opened to you. For everyone who asks receives;

he who seeks finds; and to him who knocks, the door will be opened. . . . If you then, though you are evil, know how to give good gifts to your children, how much more will your Father in heaven give the Holy Spirit to those who ask him!" (Lk 11:9-10, 13 NIV).

The spiritual power latent in local churches is largely unreleased today because clergy and laity alike expect spiritual gifts to be mainly concentrated among "full-time Christian workers." This leaves millions of laypersons operating with a self-image which does not include their gifts! This is a crippling, paralyzing illness. It harms their individual walk with God, and it robs the rest of the body of the gifts they have to contribute. Lacking a solid conviction of their full dignity as "kings and priests" (Rev 1:6 KJV), they compensate by building a self-image based on worldly success largely unrelated to the Messianic kingdom. This means that they are walking in partial darkness with respect to their own identity—a darkness the devil urgently wants to continue, because the full release of their gifts would cripple him.

Teilhard de Chardin has said that a single cell of our bodies is more complex than a star or a mountain made of unrelated grains of sand, because it is *organized* for life and productivity. Many congregations today are nothing more than transient audiences, unorganized to promote spiritual life and growth. They may have thousands in attendance but be little more than impressive heaps of sand. Some smaller congregations are *organisms* made of cellular units, small groups which are vital centers both for nurture and for new ventures of ministry.

Pastors who work toward the release and recognition of gifts among the laity and the ordering of the congregation into cellular pastoral units will find themselves freed from the intolerable burden of being the spiritual supermen who, like Atlas, are trying to hold up the whole church's ministry. No longer will they find all their time and effort drained into the black hole of the clergy-dependent local church. Instead, they will find themselves released to spend time with their families and to minister among other churches in the area or at higher denominational levels or within ecumenical networks. (The HELPER clinics run by Dr. Jerry Kirk and Ron Rand at College Hill Presbyterian Church in Cincinnati have trained many pastors in equipping the laity for ministry.[9])

This transformation of the laity is crucial for the spiritual dynamics of whole regions. Gifts and energy focused *inward* on congregations that are often homogeneous gatherings can be released to flow *outward* in ministry to other congregations in the local area that have complementary needs and gifts. Suburban churches full of affluent professionals can be linked to inner-city congregations with great financial needs and spiritual gifts that could enrich their affluent neighbors. Gifts found within the local congregation (the *microcommunity*) must be matched by a similar ordering and connection of gifts in a whole region (in the *macrocommunity;* see figure 3).

Beyond this, all the congregations in a given region ought to be linked together in prayer, planning and communication so that evangelism and social ministry can best function. If we tried to run a thousand-acre farm the way the Christian church runs local mission, we would harvest only a hundred acres' worth of crops, because the fields would be a hodgepodge of independent plantings and reapings.

John Calvin, Richard Baxter and other ecumenical Protestants have rightly insisted that only a united body of Christ in each region can effectively design and carry out ministry. When English Puritans complained to Calvin about the Anglican bishops and their popish prayer book, Calvin advised them to put up with the "tolerable stupidities" of the latter and not to trade the former for a presbyterian system. He considered it more important for the English church to stay unified than for it to adopt the polity he had drawn from the New Testament. For only a unified church can efficiently minister in any region.[10]

Even Christians who believe that microcommunities are essential to vital spirituality may draw back from the kingdom vision of a unified church in every region. They are so used to living in the tightly closed solar system of the local church that sharing gifts across congregational boundaries may be as strange to them as the idea of interstellar travel. And church leaders may be horrified at the notion of Catholics, fundamentalists, evangelicals, Pentecostals and mainline liberals talking and praying regularly together about faith and mission. Surely this must lead to theological compromise! Even more seriously, it might lead to families migrating from one congregation to another which more effectively "scratches where they itch."

Local congregations' concerns to conserve energy, combined with a sort of theological racism that fears contamination more than it loves ministry, and a jealous protectionism which fears that a transfer of members could mean a squeeze on the budget, work together against a unified church life and mission in local regions. Yet common sense and the New Testament argue strongly for unified macrocommunities in the body of Christ. Paul clearly regarded all the gatherings of Christians in a local region to be "the church" in that area. He would be appalled to find us divided up into competing teams named after favorite theologians or geographical areas!

Christians who oppose ecumenism because of their devotion to preserving the purity of one or another theological tradition must turn their minds off when they read 1 Corinthians 1:10-13 and the whole of 1 Corinthians 3. It is unfortunate that the churches which are most deeply grounded in Scripture and thus have the most help to give to other ministries are often those that draw back from ecumenical involvement in a given area. This is not simply ironic; it is a strategic coup of the devil. Jesus told us that "every kingdom divided against itself will be ruined, and every city or household divided against itself will not stand" (Mt 12:25 NIV). Jesus said this about the kingdom of darkness. But what are its implications for the kingdom of light? Satan seems to understand these much better than we do.

In a kingdom as divided as the Western church—a body broken, bruised and constricted at every point by tourniquets of division which cut off the flow of vital fluids—we hardly need to ask why a movement as numerically large as Christianity has so little influence on society and culture. But in every movement of spiritual awakening since the Reformation, parts of the shattered Messianic body have drawn together and worked across party lines in mission and ministry.

Today there are new stirrings of this impulse to unite the body of Christ. In one West Coast town, all the ministers, without exception, meet early each Sunday to pray for one another's services. In an East Coast town, all the local clergy meet monthly for strategic planning—the Catholic priest, the liberal Congregationalist, the Episcopal rector, the Orthodox Presbyterian pastor, and Methodist and Congregational evangelicals. Because of their unity, this group was able to halt a secular sex-education program in the local high school, replacing it with a four-track system embodying Catholic, Protestant, Jewish and agnostic values.

Christians are still so individualistic that they fail to understand how reaching out in mission and ecumenism will result in their own experience of a greater fullness of the Spirit and a richer atmosphere of the Spirit in their local church.

Behold, how good and pleasant it is
    when brothers dwell in unity!
It is like the precious oil upon the head,
    running down upon the beard. . . .
It is like the dew of Hermon,
    which falls on the mountains of Zion!
For there the LORD has commanded the blessing,
    life for evermore. (Ps 133)

Spurgeon, in his *Treasury of David,* comments that the Holy Spirit delights to dwell in fullness where the body of Christ is truly united.

All the images of the church in the New Testament stress the intimacy which God longs for in his relationship to his people. This relationship is as close as the one between a family and its house, or between the human spirit and the human body. A third image compares the church to the bride of the Messiah:

The king is enthralled by your beauty. . . .
All glorious is the princess within her chamber;
    her gown is interwoven with gold.
In embroidered garments she is led to the king. (Ps 45:11, 13-14 NIV)

Husbands, love your wives, just as the Messiah loved the church and gave himself up for her to make her holy . . . to present her to himself as a radiant church, without stain or wrinkle or any other blemish, but holy and blameless. (Eph 5:25-27 NIV)

A husband cannot live intimately with a wife who has been so shattered by an accident that she is in an intensive care unit. The present church lacks the presence of God's Spirit because its divisions have grieved him to the point of withdrawal. (Note that Ephesians 4:29-32 speaks of division in the body, not sin, heresy or "compromise," as the thing which "drives the Spirit from our breasts.")

The idea of "community" is very distant from laypersons, clergy and theologians when they think about improving their own spiritual lives. But this movement outward may be the quickest route to inner renewal. I once heard a black leader end an ecumenical task-force meeting with a sermon on John 17: "Jesus prays here for future Christians 'that all of them may be one, Father, just as you are in me and I am in you. May they also be in us so that the world may believe that you have sent me.' Most of our people don't care anything about church unity. In the work that we are doing, we have nothing going for us on earth. But this was Jesus' last prayer when he was on earth, and he is praying it still in heaven. And if you have Jesus praying with you, you've got a mighty powerful prayer partner!"

Theological Integration
Regional ecumenical renewal (my name for the strategy just proposed) so obviously reflects the way the church lived in the New Testament era that you may well wonder why we do not immediately start moving back toward local unified fellowship and mission. The church's present division is contrary both to Scripture and to reason. We might almost suspect that the lethal enmity and suspicion among nations may be due to the fractured condition of the church, which both models and facilitates similar divisions in the world.

As a seminary student newly converted from atheism, with no denominational background, I often asked other Christians at Peniel (the interdenominational renewal center which gave me the largest part of my spiritual and theological nurturing), "What denomination should I join?" No one wanted to give me an answer as simple as the one usually given (or implied): "mine." Instead, they told me to search the Scriptures to find which denomination was closest to the biblical model. When I did this, the Bible gave me no clear answer at all about *any* of the existing denominations (including several which claim that they alone are the true church). Instead, what it said, loud and clear, was that the whole divided state of the church was grievous and abominable to the heart of God, and that this was the fault of *all* existing churches.

Later, I discovered that one of the ways the church got divided was through individual leaders searching the Scriptures for the perfect theology or the correct way to run things. Then they either forced out of power others who did not agree with them or insisted that all true Christians follow them out of catholic wholeness into a new church of the truly orthodox. Since the Bible does not speak as clearly about theology or church polity as it does about unity, this allowed the partial doctrinal visions of generations of leaders to introduce division after division, often based primarily on economic forces, social class divisions, or the desire to build personal empires.

Even after the shattering event of the Protestant Reformation—which occurred because the Roman Catholic Church mistook a renewal movement for a band of heretics and forced out of its fellowship those whom God had raised up to reform it—Protestants like John Calvin, John Dury, Richard Baxter, Cotton Mather, and the Lutheran Pietists Philipp Jakob Spener and August Hermann Francke prayed and worked earnestly for reunion among Protestants (even while they were praying for God's judgment on "Antichrist," which had become the code word for Rome).

In the 1720s Count Ludwig von Zinzendorf, trained by the Pietists, took their teachings a step further. In founding the renewal community of Herrnhut, he deliberately made it a microcosm of the shattered body of Christ, offering shelter on his estate to many kinds of Christian refugees from the wars of religion. Moravian Hussites, Lutherans, Calvinists and even Roman Catholics came together there. At first they were continually fighting with one another—and naturally so, since Lutherans were still praying for the destruction of Calvinists in the same way Calvinists prayed for the destruction of Rome.

For three years the different sects in Herrnhut fought like cats and dogs. Zinzendorf responded by breaking the community down into small groups for sharing and prayer—landlords can do some things more readily than pastors—and escalated the volume of prayer on the

Hutberg, the mountain of God's watch, until it continued around the clock. The eventual result was Herrnhut's "Pentecost" on August 13, 1727, at a sunrise service in which all present received a powerful "baptism in the Holy Spirit." The main evidence of this outpouring on the community was the filling of members' hearts with fervent love for one another, leading to mutual forgiveness.

Only at this point did Herrnhut begin to be effective as a missionary community, exploding in outreach and far surpassing earlier Protestant evangelistic efforts. Even today many mission stations have been paralyzed by divisions and personal estrangements, and they have experienced a reviving work of the Spirit only as personal short-circuits have been rewired by mutual forgiveness.

Two kinds of mission teams went out from Herrnhut: those planting the gospel in new areas and those taking the message of spiritual renewal to the centers of existing denominations. The Pietist Spener had said that the fractured pieces of the body of Christ could not be brought together until they were spiritually renewed. Zinzendorf set about promoting renewal, seeking to draw all denominations, including Rome, together in a loose but intimate network of communication. He did not aim at the destruction of existing church bodies, but only at their closer linkage.

Zinzendorf felt that every existing denomination reflects a particular style of worship, order, spirituality and theology which ought to be permitted in the reunited body of Christ, without being restrained or forced away. Every church has its jewel of truth to express; and jewels must be gathered, not forced together in a way that obscures their luster. Zinzendorf's concept of ecumenicity could be summed up by Richard Baxter's phrase, "unity without uniformity."

What about the bond of doctrinal truth uniting the different gift-bearing segments of Christ's body? As a layperson, Zinzendorf did not know enough traditional theology to confuse him. He felt that "the essentials of the Gospel may be written on a single sheet of paper in large handwriting."[11] He did not rule out the necessity to construct more complex systems of doctrinal understanding. But as a mission theorist and ecumenist, he was primarily concerned that both converts and professing Christians should concentrate on the core of the gospel, "the adoration of the Lamb of God," and that they should know "the death of Christ upon the heart."[12]

It would be easy to conclude from this kind of pattern—as both Protestant liberals and fundamentalists have done—that theology is a divisive nuisance. Some think that theologians should be kept in reservations (like seminaries). There they can amuse themselves harmlessly by making generations of students jump through systematic hoops for a few years before graduating, thawing out and eventually learning how to apply the simple gospel. Some might suppose that *all* extended theological systems are what Luther called "theologies of glory." Such theologies venture beyond what we can really know about God and seek to psychoanalyze his motives or to catch his mind and will in a philosophical net. Why not eschew all theological systems, declare allegiance to "No creeds but the Bible," and simply entrust our minds and wills to the guidance of the Holy Spirit speaking through Scripture alone?

This is initially plausible. Systems which relate biblical truth to the world soon grow partially obsolete, as did Thomas Aquinas's great synthesis between Aristotelian philosophy and Augustinian theology. And theological systems are often irrelevant to the deepest needs of the heart, which demand truth focused on existential needs. Kierkegaard said of Hegel, "I asked him for a street guide to Copenhagen, and he gave me a map of Europe!"

It can also be argued that reformation and renewal never take place apart from Christians coming out from behind the shelter of their doctrinal systems to encounter Scripture directly. Theology is one step removed from biblical revelation. It can domesticate or rationalize our knowledge of God, "teaching as doctrines the precepts of men" (Mk 7:7). And there is a dead, rote quality to faith based on hearsay rather than on firsthand exposure to divine revelation. What I call "Xerox theology"—theology that fails to relate Scripture directly to current needs and conditions but is content to pass on a doctrinal inheritance tailored to events in another century—can be dangerously misleading. Charts of the shifting conditions where rivers meet the sea must be constantly updated. Otherwise they will send us away from the main channel and into the sand bars.

When I first became a Christian, I found my head full of conflicting authorities and directives. My mind was a sea of ideas I had learned from mystics, theologians, psychologists and philosophers, with a little knowledge of Scripture floating among the other items. When I asked my spiritual mentor at that time, Donald Mostrom, how to order this doctrinal chaos, he took down a copy of Calvin's *Institutes*. But he did *not* say, "Simply believe this." Instead, he commended the theological *method* of Calvin: "Suspend everything you have been taught, for the moment (including the ideas of Donald Mostrom!), and begin to pore through the text of Scripture, depending on the Holy Spirit to validate what is true and reject what is false, rebuilding and refurnishing your mind."

The next several years were filled with spiritual excitement as I encountered biblical truth with a sense of joy and immediacy in the atmosphere of the Spirit's presence. I learned much also from history and tradition. But the Scripture forced this material in new directions, dissolving inherited problems and raising other issues.

Initially it was as though I had taken the entire contents of my Yale education and dumped it out of my mind, as we dump broken furniture on the lawn during clean-up week. Then, year by year, with some encouragement from mentors, I went out to the lawn, where everything remained uncollected, and brought items back into the mind's household, arranging them as Scripture directed. Eventually that household contained furniture far beyond the text of the Bible. But my aim was that the ruling voice in selecting and ordering ideas should always be *the Holy Spirit speaking through the Word.*

This idea of *biblical integration of learning* has been a critical need since the Reformation. The Reformers avoided the encyclopedic system building of medieval scholasticism, concentrating on refining the redemptive core of theology: Christology and the doctrines of sin, grace and salvation. But their descendants in the next century, the Puritan encyclopedists and the Moravian Jan Comenius (who founded Western educational theory), sought to retain a God-centered order among the new disciplines emerging from the use of reason and scientific method. Thinkers like Edwards and Timothy Dwight were able to counter the intellectual threat of the eighteenth-century. Enlightenment, which forged a humanistic understanding of reality. Divergent but powerfully disturbing challenges in the next century, from geniuses like Darwin, Marx and Freud, paved the way for the secular humanism of our own time. These forces remain strong in the ruling centers of Western society, even though their implications are increasingly seen to be dehumanizing.

Historian Timothy Smith has said that while Catholics and Protestants were fighting each other in America at the end of the nineteenth century, the humanists took over the educational system. Generations of Christian minds have gone through the Waring blender of this system. As a result, they have become *destructively enculturated* through the admixture of secular notions thus producing the various forms of modernist theology. Half the American church opted out of this system in the early part of this century, electing to bury its head in Bible schools rather than fight the forces of secular learning on their own ground. This strategy has produced *protective enculturation* among fundamentalists, enclosing a safe but frozen and isolated mental universe.

Christianity has continued to grow even under these conditions, just as it thrives in spite of political tyranny behind the Iron Curtain. But the church has largely either evaded or capitulated to an intellectual attack that has dismissed Christianity as a harmless delusion. Such a church cannot leaven society with kingdom values. What is needed to move our culture into some measure of conformity to God's will is God-centered and kingdom-centered thinking. And we do not do much of this in the church. Christians who cultivate the spiritual life have come to be anti-intellectual, as Richard Hofstadter points out; while those who value culture have too often become estranged both from spiritual growth and from biblical truth.[13]

This dichotomy points us to the pressing need for theological integration. Despite the divisive effect of dead scholasticism, an absolute biblicism divorced from tradition and system is even more dangerous. Beyond the extremes of cool rationalism and mindless enthusiasm, the church needs *Spirit-filled minds*.

We do not often realize that the early church was saved from remaining a Jewish sect, or from dissolving into paganism by accommodation, through the work of a great theologian. Paul was able to lead the early church between the polar dangers of protective and destructive enculturation. We need to pray today that God will raise up counterparts to Paul and Augustine and Luther and Edwards and Kuyper, spiritually energized thinkers who can steer between the twin dangers of obscurantism and sophistication.

Since the rise of the counterculture of the 1960s, there are signs that Western society is reacting away from technocracy and secular humanism in a religious direction. Christianity, other world religions, cults and even pagan witchcraft are live options for the new bull market in religion. The shift from the Industrial Age to the Age of Information may facilitate widespread spiritual awakening, just as the printing press paved the way for the Reformation. Previous awakenings have traveled with the spread of news about what God was doing. We are entering an era when it will be difficult to block the dissemination of any kind of truth.

But the very deluge of new information can make the task of integration harder. Imagine that you are standing before a robot with eight arms, each of which is constantly pitching citrus fruit—lemons, oranges, grapefruit—and also an occasional hand grenade. Your task is to catch all of these, sorting the fruit and discarding the grenades. The robot is pitching four times the number of items you can handle with your two hands.

This is what life feels like in many college classrooms. But nearly all of us experience the trauma of the information explosion. New facts and interpretations—and pseudofacts that later self-destruct or demonic lies that may explode our faith—are coming at us at a speed almost too fast for us to sort and integrate. No wonder Western Christians either build thought systems with dangerous antibiblical elements (destructive enculturation), or offer us neat, simple inherited boxes with little or no fruit in them, because they have moved out of range of the robot (protective enculturation).

How can we handle the task of integrating this deluge of ideas? Let me offer a few suggestions:

1. We must first be convinced that theological integration is not an irrelevant frill in Christian life and mission. It is essential to spiritual

health and theological sanity. Without it, our society will inevitably fall into the hands of those who understand the force of ideology in culture. It is no accident that when Communists want to take over a nation, they invade the key centers of its thinking—universities and media. Evangelical Christianity has been losing Western society, not for want of numbers or strong ideas, but because it systematically starves its brain cells while spending billions on evangelistic outreach. We cannot slacken the pace of evangelism. But we must go back to the expensive task the Reformers and the Puritans did not shirk: building a truly *Christian* humanism. Just as in every previous spiritual awakening, we are going to have to spend significant amounts of money on *education*—building new schools at every level and recapturing older institutions that were founded to support the kingdom.

2. As individuals we need to invest time in two kinds of background study. First, we need to move out in theological integration. We need to pore through the text of Scripture repeatedly, allowing the Holy Spirit to rebuild our minds and confront our spiritual needs (for a renewed mind is ineffective, or even dangerous, without a renewed life). Second, we need to study theology, because the systems formed in the past *do* have relevance for the present. Modern theologians have repeated the most elementary errors because they have failed to study carefully the history of doctrine. The core of Christian faith in the historic creeds and confessions of the church cannot be ignored without denaturing the gospel. In their central utterances, the great theological traditions stemming from Augustine, Luther, Calvin, the evangelical Anabaptists, Wesley, and the later fundamentalists and Pentecostals are in agreement. Apart from that core, each contains elements that may appear to be in conflict but are actually complementary, like the differing sound images in multichannel music systems. The church of the future will not anchor the church irrevocably to any of these traditions, but will allow all to interact significantly to enrich the church.

3. This could mean that laypersons may need to invest several years in formal theological training. Extension programs from seminaries will make this increasingly necessary and feasible. Meanwhile, churches need to involve laypersons in courses of study, like the

Bethel Series, that offer theology with a practical focus. These may not be at the academic level of the seminary, but the information they provide may be spiritually and theologically more enlivening and accessible.

I am more and more convinced that Christianity has lost control of Western culture because it has failed to spend time and money on the cultivation of the mind. The result is a modernism that cannot transform culture because it has capitulated to paganism, and a fundamentalism which has no traction because it is out of touch. The only way we can avoid these polar dangers of destructive and protective enculturation is to invest time, money and prayer where the impact is greatest: in the formation of Christian hearts and minds. Warm hearts alone will not conquer a culture unless we wield the instruments that govern the central mindset of society: *ideas*. But ideas alone will be powerless unless they are controlled and directed by Spirit-filled hearts.

As I look out on American Christianity, I see a movement which is fantastically enlarged at some points and dwarfed in others. It is like the caricatures we see in funhouse mirrors: a small head and a huge mouth, a tiny torso and immense hands and feet. This may be simple immaturity. A baby's limbs are also out of proportion. Still, it will take time, effort and prayer to change this picture so that the world will see not a strange sort of monster, but the glorious bride of Christ. And this means that it will also take economic resources. But these will be forthcoming. Every past spiritual awakening has involved the release of the gifts of laity to do the primary work of mission. We can expect the appearance soon of God- and kingdom-centered laypersons who will plunge their lives and fortunes unreservedly into the Messianic enterprise.

I grew up in Albuquerque, New Mexico, where the landscape is dominated by two things: the desert and the Rio Grande. Between the two is a fertile area made fruitful by irrigation canals carrying water from the river. If it were not for the canals, the desert would close in and many persons would starve.

In *God Bless You, Mr. Rosewater*, Kurt Vonnegut talks about "the money river," describing a lawyer who is always looking for a way to get a bucket into the economic stream that enriches society.[14] The church has sometimes tapped into the money river in ways which have destroyed the force of its institutions, flooding its basements instead of irrigating the desert. Today it has only partially avoided this problem. But it has only begun to release the financial energy, along with all the other gifts, which are locked within the laity.

The life-giving force of Christianity in history is symbolized in Ezekiel 47 by a small stream emerging from the second temple. The stream rapidly deepens and broadens until it becomes a great river which causes the desert to blossom with the rose, and heals the Dead Sea so that it swarms with fish. There are seasons in which all rivers become narrow and shallower. The Rio Grande in winter is a thin ribbon of water surrounded by a wide mud flat. This is a picture of much of the church today: a dry riverbed filled with shapes of earth carved once by the force of living waters.

But with every spring, the torrents flow in the arroyos, and the river and its canals are filled again with the fluid of life. Every river grows larger as it approaches the sea. As we move toward the end of the twentieth century and the end of history, do not pray only for your own spiritual renewal. Pray for a springtime of the Spirit which will enrich the church and the world, an awakening for which all earlier renewal movements have been only rehearsals.

Discussion Questions

Recommended supplemental reading: chapter 5 in *Dynamics*. Scripture for meditation: Acts 1—4; 1 Corinthians 2.

Section 1: Mission

1. In your experience, how mission-conscious are Christians today? Why do churches find it hard to focus on mission?

2. What problems do you find in witnessing to others about Christ? What solutions for these problems have you found?

3. How important is it for Christians to get a perspective on the spiritual and physical needs of the whole world? How can we go about it?

4. Do you believe the Christian church should be an agent in transforming American society? What does this have to do with world evangelistic mission?

5. How can we best resolve the differences between Christians who emphasize only evangelism and those who stress changing society?

6. What is the relationship between kingdom-centered living and world mission (understood both as evangelistic and social ministry)?

Section 2: Prayer

1. God already knows our needs. Why is it important for our Christian lives that we voice them in prayer?

2. How can we avoid being so general in prayer that it becomes boring and irrelevant, or so specific that it seems like work? Is there any single pattern we should follow in prayer?

3. What is the connection between prayer and Christ's present ministry on our behalf?

4. Why are private and corporate prayer both vital for spiritual life?

5. How can we make our prayers less self-centered and more kingdom-centered?

6. As you think of your own life and the Christian groups in which you are involved, where is more prayer needed?

Section 3: Community

1. Do you think our culture promotes self-centeredness or supports community? In what ways?

2. How do the images of the church in Scripture emphasize the importance of community?

3. Why have Protestants had so much difficulty seeing the importance of community?

4. In your experience, does the average church properly fulfill the need for Christian community? How could this be changed?

5. How conscious is the average Christian of his or her gifts for the rest of the body of Christ? How can we change this?

6. How important is "the ecumenical movement" of this century? In what ways should this be a matter for our further prayer and action?

Section 4: Theological Integration

1. Why is the need for theological integration at the root of divisions in the church? How can we resolve these divisions?

2. Can we prove from the Scripture that theology and theologians are really important? Why isn't the Bible enough?

3. What is the key to keeping theology fresh, relevant and vital?

4. If the Bible's truth is always constant, why does theology constantly need revision and renewal?

5. How can we be consistently Christian in our thinking when we are constantly bombarded by slanted chains of reasoning?

6. How does the whole process of education need to be changed in order to produce Spirit-filled Christian minds?

Appendix A
The Mind's Eye

The accompanying diagrams illustrate the progress of renewal in Christian growth. They represent the various fields of vision for people at different levels of Christian maturity. Each may be useful as a focus of meditation. Scripture passages listed below each figure shed light on the significance of each diagram.

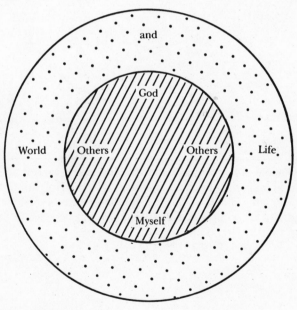

Figure 1
The Mind's Eye: Blinded by Sin

Figure 1 portrays the mind and heart of persons rejecting the true God and his Son the Messiah (Rom 1:18-22). It may also symbolize the darkened condition of the mind in Christian believers who are not walking in the light (Eph 4:17-19).

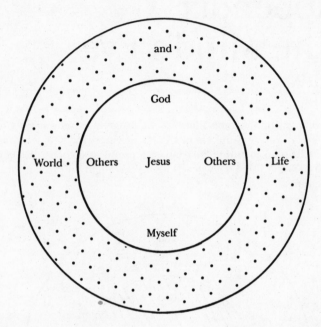

Figure 2
The Mind's Eye: Convicted and Illuminated

Figure 2 symbolizes the central understanding at the root of all thinking, feeling and willing which has been illuminated by the Holy Spirit (Eph 1:15-23). This new clarity of vision gives us a deep awareness of the holy God and of sin, and also the confidence that the great gap between us and God's holiness is bridged by Jesus the Messiah.

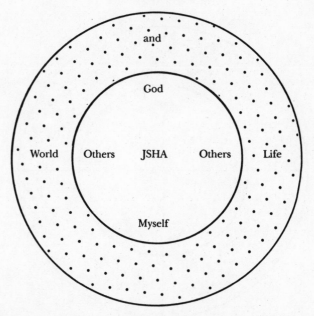

Figure 3
The Mind's Eye: Dynamics of Personal Renewal

Figure 3 spells out the benefits obtained for us by Jesus the Messiah in his Incarnation, sacrificial death and resurrection. These benefits are symbolized by the four letters JSHA (an acronym for *Yeshua,* the Hebrew form of Jesus' name which means "Jehovah is deliverance"). JSHA unfolds for us the content of Jesus' delivering work: *justification* (Rom 5:1-11), *sanctification* (Rom 6:1-18), the *Holy Spirit's indwelling* (Rom 8:1-27), and *authority in spiritual warfare* (Jas 4:7).

Theological Integration

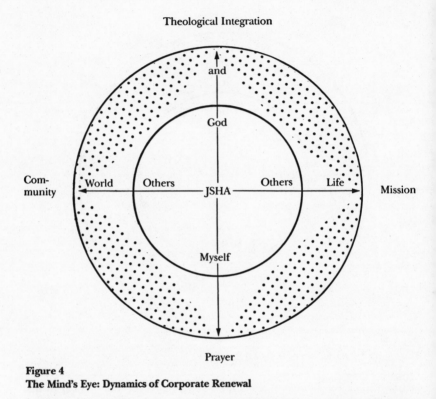

Figure 4
The Mind's Eye: Dynamics of Corporate Renewal

Figure 4 pictures the outworking of our deliverance beyond the individual level. Maximum spiritual growth requires vigorous involvement in *mission* (Acts 1:6-8), waiting on God in corporate *prayer* (Acts 1:13-14), participation in *community* (Acts 2:42-47) and the renewing of our minds to reflect the mind of Christ (1 Cor 2)—*theological integration.* All of these centrifugal movements sweep out from the central core of renewal to clear our minds and our world from the works of darkness.

Appendix B
The Foundation for Church Renewal

To help direct resources where they are needed, I have joined with several laypeople with development gifts in the creation of the *Foundation for Church Renewal*. This foundation is devoted to channeling resources to neglected areas of the body of Christ with precious gifts for ministry, but little economic support. We support ministries which promote theological reformation and denominational renewal, Christian education, Christian artists in all genres, media ministries employing these, spiritual dynamics training, Christian unity on the basis of evangelical faith, mission and evangelism in neglected forms, evangelical social ministries, and prayer/study forums in Washington and elsewhere.

Please pray for the work of the Foundation for Church Renewal, which summarizes in its work the whole thrust of this book, culminating in the empowering of the Christian mind. Its goal is a Messianic movement which can demonstrate the force of the kingdom in ordinary history, because it has grown to the full stature of maturity. If you have funds to invest in the renewal of the Christian enterprise, the Foundation can help you channel these to crucial ministries. In addition to its work in funding and development, the Foundation publishes my quarterly newsletter, *Renewal*, which seeks to track the course of renewal in the Western church. A year's subscription to the *Renewal* newsletter can be obtained by sending the Foundation a tax-deductible donation. The address of the Foundation for Church Renewal is P.O. Box 2337, South Hamilton, MA 01982.

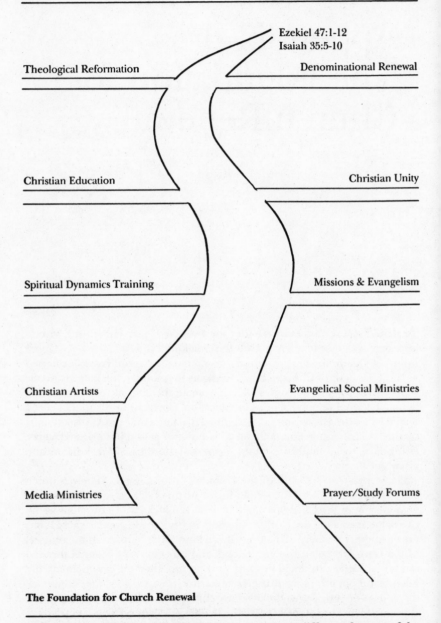

Ezekiel 47:1-12
Isaiah 35:5-10

Theological Reformation

Denominational Renewal

Christian Education

Christian Unity

Spiritual Dynamics Training

Missions & Evangelism

Christian Artists

Evangelical Social Ministries

Media Ministries

Prayer/Study Forums

The Foundation for Church Renewal

This diagram of a river and its tributaries represents different focuses of the Foundation and how they come together to bring renewal to the church.

Notes

Chapter 1: The God-Centered Life

[1]Willis W. Harmon, "Notes on the Coming Transformation," in Andrew A. Spekke, ed., *The Next 25 Years: Crisis & Opportunity* (Washington, D.C.: World Future Society, 1975).

[2]*U.S. News and World Report* 82, no. 14 (11 April 1977): 54-72.

[3]"Report of the Vocation Agency," *Minutes of the 193rd General Assembly of the United Presbyterian Church in the U.S.A.* (1981), pp. 426-27, 446-58.

[4]Roger Martin, "An Evangelical Chair at Harvard," *Christianity Today* 27, no. 3 (4 February 1983): 14-16.

[5]*New York Times*, 12 March 1982.

[6]*Missionscope*, March 1980, p. 1.

[7]*Wall Street Journal*, 11 July 1980, p. 1.

[8]See chapter 8, "How Revivals Go Wrong," in my *Dynamics of Spiritual Life* (Downers Grove, Ill.: InterVarsity Press, 1979).

[9]John of the Cross, *The Dark Night of the Soul*, trans. Kurt Reinhardt (New York: Frederick Ungar, 1957), pt. 1, bk. 1, chaps. 2-7.

[10]Augustine *Confessions* 13. 9.

[11]Tom Wolfe, "The Me Decade," *New York Magazine*, 27 August 1976.

[12]John Calvin *Institutes* 1. 1. 1.

[13]Rudolf Otto, *The Idea of the Holy* (Oxford: Oxford University Press, 1928), pp. 12-41.

[14]Calvin *Institutes* 1. 1. 2.

[15]Johann Tauler, *Signposts to Perfection*, ed. Elizabeth Strakosch (St. Louis: B. Herder, 1958), pp. 99-100.

[16]W. H. Auden, "For the Time Being: A Christmas Oratorio," *The Collected Poetry of W. H. Auden* (New York: Random House, 1945), p. 411.

[17]Jonathan Edwards, "Personal Narrative," as cited in Sereno Dwight's "Memoirs of Jonathan Edwards," in *The Works of Jonathan Edwards*, ed. Sereno Dwight, 2 vols. (Edinburgh, Scotland: Banner of Truth Trust, 1974), 1:lv.

[18]Ibid.

[19]Ibid., pp. lxxxix-xc.

[20]Jonathan Edwards, "Some Thoughts Concerning the Revival," *Jonathan Edwards: The Great Awakening*, ed. C. C. Goen (New Haven: Yale University Press, 1972), pp. 336-440.

[21]Augustine, *Treatise on I John IV, 6*, cited in Thomas Hand, *St. Augustine on Prayer* (Westminster, Md.: Newman Press, 1963), p. 8.

[22]Augustine *Confessions* 1. 1.

[23]Augustine *Confessions* 10. 27.

[24]Augustine, *On Ps. 76:2*, cited in Hand, *Augustine on Prayer*, p. 51.

[25]Augustine, *Sermon 33*, cited in ibid., p. 75.

[26]Augustine, *Tr. on Ps. 2*, cited in ibid., p. 52.

[27]Augustine, *On Ps. 39:7, 8*, cited in ibid.

[28]Augustine, *Sermon 256*, cited in ibid., p. 127.

[29]Augustine, *On Ps. 26*, cited in ibid., p. 126.

[30]Augustine, *The City of God*, cited in ibid.

[31]Augustine, *Sermon 252*, cited in ibid., p. 128.

[32]Augustine, *Sermon 255*, cited in ibid., p. 129.

[33]Augustine, *On Ps. 84*, cited in ibid.

[34]*Westminster Larger Catechism*, question 1.

Chapter 2: The Kingdom-Centered Life

[1]Franz Delitzsch and C. F. Keil, *Biblical Commentary on the Old Testament* (Grand Rapids: Eerdmans, 1956), 2:183-84.

[2]See, for example, Karl Holl, *The Cultural Significance of the Reformation*, trans. Karl and Barbara Hertz and John H. Lichtblau (New York: Meridian Books, 1959).

[3]This is the thesis of H. Richard Niebuhr's *The Kingdom of God in America* (New York: Willett, Clark & Co., 1937).

[4]For a critique of the Weber-Tawney thesis, see Kurt Samuelsson, *Religion and Economic Action* (New York: Harper & Row, 1957).

[5]Edmund S. Morgan, *The Puritan Family* (New York: Harper & Row, 1944), chap. 7.

[6]Cotton Mather, *Magnalia Christi Americana* (London, 1702), 1:63.

[7]Lisa Birnbach, ed., *The Official Preppy Handbook* (New York: Workman Publishers, 1980).

[8]Niebuhr, *Kingdom of God in America*, pp. 36-44.

[9]Richard Hutcheson's manuscript, whose current working title is *The Lay Revolution*, will be published in 1985.

[10]See J. A. De Jong, *As the Waters Cover the Sea: Millennial Expectations in the Rise of Anglo-American Missions 1640-1810* (Kampen, the Netherlands: J. H. Kok, 1970); and Iain Murray, *The Puritan Hope* (London: Banner of Truth Trust, 1971).

[11]Erich Beyreuther, *August Hermann Francke und die Anfange der Dekumenischen Bewegung* (Hamburg, Germany: Herbert Reich Evang. Verlag, 1957), pp. 30-31, 50.

[12]See Timothy L. Smith, *Revivalism and Social Reform in Mid-Nineteenth-Century America* (New York: Abingdon Press, 1957); Howard Snyder, *The Radical Wesley* (Downers Grove, Ill.: InterVarsity Press, 1980); and Donald Dayton, *Discovering an Evangelical Heritage* (New York: Harper & Row, 1976).

[13]See Charles I. Foster, *An Errand of Mercy* (Chapel Hill, N.C.: University of North Carolina Press, 1960).

[14]For an account of the Clapham movement, see E. M. Howse, *Saints in Politics* (Toronto: University of Toronto Press, 1952).

[15]See Ford K. Brown, *Fathers of the Victorians: The Age of Wilberforce* (Cambridge: Cambridge University Press, 1961).

[16]Charles C. Cole, Jr., *The Social Ideas of the Northern Evangelists* (New York: Octagon Books, 1966), pp. 102-3.

[17]Alexis de Tocqueville, *Democracy in America*, 2 vols. (New York: Vintage Books, 1945), 1:314; Philip Schaff, *America* (New York: Scribner, 1854), pp. 94, 118.

[18]See Robert T. Handy, *America's Religious Depression 1925-1935* (Philadelphia: Fortress Press, 1968).

Chapter 3: The Flesh

[1]Donald G. Mostrom, *The Dynamics of Intimacy with God* (Wheaton, Ill.: Tyndale, 1983), pp. 43-77.

[2]Walter Rauschenbusch, *A Theology for the Social Gospel* (New York: Macmillan, 1917), pp. 77-94.

[3]Edwards, "Some Thoughts," p. 418.

[4]Martin Luther, "Explanations of the 95 Theses," in *Luther's Works*, vol. 31, ed. Harold J. Grimm (Philadelphia: Muhlenberg Press, 1957), pp. 128-30.

[5]Gerard Manley Hopkins, "That Nature is a Heraclitean Fire and of the comfort of the Resurrection," *The Poems of Gerard Manley Hopkins*, 4th ed., ed. W. H. Gardner and N. H. MacKenzie (New York: Oxford University Press, 1967), pp. 105-6.

Chapter 4: The World

[1]Shirley Jackson, *The Haunting of Hill House* (New York: Viking Press, 1959).

[2]Allen Ginsberg, *Howl* (San Francisco: City Light Books, 1956), p. 17.

Chapter 5: The Devil

[1]Rauschenbusch, *A Theology for the Social Gospel*, pp. 77-94.

[2]C. S. Lewis, *That Hideous Strength* (New York: Macmillan, 1946).

[3]*Life Magazine*, 2 February 1948, p. 77.

[4]Cotton Mather, *Icono-Clastes* (Boston, 1717), preface.

Chapter 6: The Messianic Victory

[1]T. S. Eliot, *Murder in the Cathedral* (London: Faber and Faber, 1935), p. 52.

[2]William Golding, *Lord of the Flies* (New York: G. B. Putnam, 1978).

Chapter 7: Dynamics of Individual Renewal

[1]P. T. Forsyth, *Christian Perfection* (London: Hodder and Stoughton, n.d.), pp. 55-56.

[2]Ibid., pp. 16-17.

[3]Ibid., pp. 7-10.

[4]T. S. Eliot, "Burnt Norton," *Four Quartets* (New York: Harcourt, Brace and World, 1971), pp. 42-43.

[5]Forsyth, *Christian Perfection*, pp. 68, 71, 74-75.

[6]See Ernest Gordon Rupp, *The Righteousness of God* (London: Hodder and Stoughton, 1953), chap. 6.

[7]Dietrich Bonhoeffer, *The Cost of Discipleship* (New York: Macmillan, 1959), pp. 35-47.

[8]Jeremy Rifkin, *The Emerging Order: God in the Age of Scarcity* (New York: G. P. Putnam's Sons, 1979), chaps. 8-11.

[9]John Livingston Nevius, *Demon Possession and Allied Themes* (Old Tappan, N.J.: Revell, 1894), pp. 75-76, 129-31.

Chapter 8: Dynamics of Corporate Renewal

[1]Further information can be obtained from U.S. Center for World Missions, 1605 E. Elizabeth St., Pasadena, CA 91104.

[2]Richard Hutcheson, *The Lay Revolution;* also see Roberta H. Winter, *Once More around Jericho* (Pasadena: William Carey Library, 1978).

[3]J. Christy Wilson, *Today's Tentmakers* (Wheaton, Ill.: Tyndale, 1979).

[4]Jeremy Rifkin, *Algeny* (New York: Viking Press, 1983), pp. 61-156.

[5]Alvin Toffler, *The Third Wave* (New York: William Morrow and Co., 1980), chap. 18.

[6]Reinhold Niebuhr, *Moral Man and Immoral Society* (New York: Charles Scribner's Sons, 1932).

[7]Further information may be obtained from Evangelicals for Social Action, P.O. Box 76560, Washington, D.C. 20013.

[8]David Bryant, *In the Gap: What It Means to Be a World Christian* (Ventura, Calif.: Regal, 1984); *With Concerts of Prayer* (Ventura, Calif.: Regal, 1984).

[9]The HELPER Clinic can be contacted at College Hill Presbyterian Church, 5742 Hamilton Ave., Cincinnati, OH 45224.

[10]John T. McNeill, "The Ecumenical Idea and Efforts to Realize It, 1517-1618," *A History of the Ecumenical Movement*, vol. 1, ed. Ruth Rouse and Stephen C. Neill (London: S.P.C.K., 1953), pp. 27-69.

[11]A. J. Lewis, *Zinzendorf the Ecumenical Pioneer* (London: SCM Press, 1962), p. 15. This is the best popular account for background on Zinzendorf and Herrnhut.

[12]Ibid.

[13]See Richard Hofstadter, *Anti-Intellectualism in America* (New York: Alfred A. Knopf, 1963).

[14]Kurt Vonnegut, *God Bless You, Mr. Rosewater* (New York: Delacorte, 1971), chap. 1.

Index